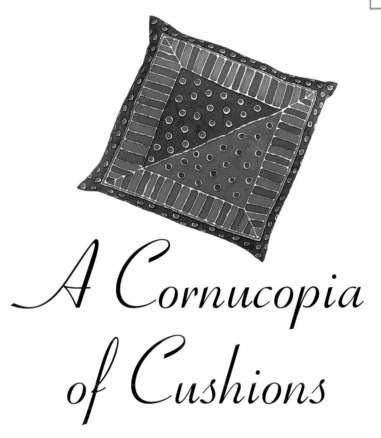

A Cornucopia
of Cushions

A Cornucopia of Cushions

40 Inspiring Projects to Grace Your Home

Susie Johns

APPLE

A QUARTO BOOK

Published by the Apple Press
6 Blundell Street
London N7 9BH

ISBN 1 85076 766 1

This book was designed and produced by
Quarto Publishing plc
The Old Brewery
6 Blundell Street
London N7 9BH

Senior art editor Clare Baggaley
Designer Tanya Devonshire-Jones
Editors Sarah Fergusson, Miranda Stoner,
   Jo Fletcher-Watson
Text editor Maggie McCormick
Managing editor Sally MacEachern
Photographer Laura Wickenden
Illustrator Lesley Wakerley
Picture researcher Miriam Hyman
Picture research manager Giulia
   Hetherington
Assistant art director Penny Cobb
Art Director Moira Clinch
Editorial director Mark Dartford

Typeset by Type Technique, London W1
Manufactured in Singapore by
Universal Graphics Pte Ltd
Printed in Singapore by
Star Standard Industries (Pte) Ltd

Contents

Country   18

Pretty Pillows

Pillows can add the finishing touch or be an intrinsic part of a home-decorating plan. They can be functional or fancy, firm and supportive, or soft and yielding. They can be almost any shape or size and covered in almost any kind of fabric. Put them on a chair seat, arrange them on a sofa, scatter them around.

Most chairs and sofas can be improved in comfort or appearance – or both – by the addition of pillows. Decide on the style or image you want to create and use pillows to enhance existing furnishings or to make changes. After all, it is easier to re-cover a few pillows than it is to reupholster a sofa.

You can use pillows and cushions in any room in the house. During the day, a group of pretty pillows on a neatly made bed looks lovely; at night, they provide extra support for reading in bed. In the kitchen or dining room, soften the seats of hard chairs with squab cushions, tied in place. In the backyard or on the deck, use box-shaped cushions for benches or wicker furniture. In the playroom or den, make large cushions to put on the floor, or doll-sized ones for scaled-down furniture.

There are 40 projects in this book, offering a wide selection of designs that can be adapted to different purposes, different rooms, different homes, different lifestyles. Some are quick and simple to make; others are moderately easy, requiring only basic sewing skills, while some offer the opportunity for creativity, the chance to try out new techniques, perhaps, and above all the inspiration to create a unique piece for your own home.

The book is divided into five chapters: Country, Exotic, Victorian, Four Corners, and Contemporary. Your home may fall into one of these categories. But the groups are just a device: a Victorian-style pillow may be ideal for your all-white contemporary bedroom, while a country-style seat cushion could look great made up in fabric to match your living-room curtains.

Country

Whether we live in the city or in rural isolation, in a cozy cottage or a high-rise apartment, many of us are country folk at heart – at least in our choice of decoration. While there is no denying that floral fabrics, ginghams, and ruffles look right at home in a country kitchen or living room, they can also add the right touch of hominess and contentment to almost any situation.

So if you have a liking for homespun cloth, patchwork, home-baked cookies, farmhouse furniture, and rag rugs, you'll want to make pillows that are informal, casual, and pretty. Mix and match is one of the keys to this look: don't go for coordinated fabrics, matching trimmings, and careful color scheming. Instead, raid your rag bag, salvage scraps, and put together diverse patterns and colors. Patchwork has a wonderful way of uniting an indifferent array of fabric scraps. Appliqué, too, is a carefree craft where the scrawniest scrap can become part of a treasured heirloom!

Make seat cushions – squabs – for all your hard chairs, but use a variety of fabrics. Rescue that patchwork quilt you started to make but abandoned when it was only a foot square – it'll make a lovely cover! Discover the craft of appliqué if you haven't already done so; stitch a needlepoint panel or crochet a lace edging.

Exotic

They are irresistible, aren't they? Those rich, sumptuous fabrics – velvet, brocade, silk, satin, and shimmering metallics. This may be the style you choose for your whole house, a whole room, or just one corner: rich, floor-length drapes, an abundance of fabric, comfort, opulence, and indulgence. Of course, just a plain old couch, bed, or chair can be given the exotic treatment simply by re-covering pillows with splendid fabrics.

If this is a style that attracts you, your first priority will probably not be laundry. You may, however, want to bear in mind whether the deluxe fabrics you choose can be washed or drycleaned. If your velvet pillows and bolsters are to be lounged upon daily, choose a washable cotton velveteen. If they are just for show, you can allow yourself to be influenced by the glorious colors and textures and not worry so much about how to remove spills!

This is a category for show-offs, too, so it is likely you are turned on by color and image as well as fabrics that are tactile. When creating pillows, then, why not juxtapose vibrant colors, incorporate symbolism, and introduce an element of surprise!

Victorian

Although 19th-century furniture tended to be heavily upholstered, the Victorians still liked to indulge their passion for comfort by adding pillows. There were frills and ruffles in the morning room, brocades and velvets in the drawing room. And Victorian ladies delighted in showing off their needlework skills – so if this is the look you want to create in your home, there is ample opportunity for indulging yourself with embroidery, needlepoint, and patchwork.

One way to get the look is to buy old fabrics and turn them into covers. A small piece of needlepoint or crewelwork found in a thrift store or flea market, even if it is in bad repair, can be salvaged and applied to a fabric backing. If you are starting from scratch, however, by choosing velvets and brocades and pairing them with the right style of trimming, you can create a modern pillow with a Victorian look. You can also try your hand at needlepoint – designs that incorporate fruit and flowers can create an authentic feel – or work a cross-stitch sampler and turn it into a pillow instead of framing it to hang on the wall. For a bedroom, what could be more unashamedly pretty than a pile of pillows in crisp white cotton and edged with eyelet lace like Victorian petticoats?

Four Corners

When seeking inspiration for designs, there are rich examples to be found in different cultures. Embroidery, fabric painting and printing, weaving, and dyeing are crafts that are practiced the world over with very exciting results. If you are tired of floral chintz, if you want to get in touch with your primitive self, or if you prefer to fill your home with natural materials, then perhaps you need to look in a far-flung corner of the globe for inspiration.

Ethnic style means different things to different people, of course. Natural does not mean lacking in color – far from it! If you have furnished your home with rattan furniture and rush matting, stripped wood and basketware, you may want to continue the theme with an Indonesian-style batik pillow in authentic shades of brown and black. On the other hand, a touch of bold, bright color with its roots in Africa, India, or Central America may be just what you need. Paint it, stitch it, or even knit it!

If there is one thing that epitomizes an up-to-date interior, it has to be lack of clutter. In this definition, however, "clutter" does not extend to pillows! Furniture with clean lines, in a no-fuss environment, is just the place to display your creative skills to their best advantage. Many traditional crafts – patchwork, fabric printing, and appliqué – can be carried into the 21st century. It is not the technique that counts, but the way it is applied, the colors and designs, the final effect.

Once you have decided on your color scheme and furniture, you can play with objects and arrangements – a few pillows or many, or a single statement. When creating pillows for a modern home, fine art is a good starting point for design. The paintings of Mondrian, Matisse, Robert Motherwell, or Jasper Johns provide excellent templates for fabric and thread. If you are unsure, experiment with bright color combinations in the playroom first. Let the children create their own slipcovers by painting directly on fabric: once you see how easy it is to obtain sensational effects, you'll want to try it for yourself.

Fabrics

There are no right or wrong choices in the types of fabric to use for making pillows. Some are more hard-wearing, easier to clean, and care for – but ultimately the choice is yours. If you want to create an exotic ambience, there is little point in recommending gingham and muslin. The rule is – there are no rules! However, don't expect a fine silk, or a novelty lamé, to stand up to too much wear and tear.

Faille is a fine, plain weave with a characteristic crosswise rib, woven from silk, acetate, viscose, or polyester.

Linen is a natural fabric made from flax fibers and often blended with cotton to make hard-wearing upholstery fabrics. It is liable to crease, but wonderful to work with, especially with embroidery.

Gingham has a characteristic checked weave, combining white with colored threads. Pure cotton gingham, intended for dressmaking, is excellent for patchwork and appliqué, and lovely color effects can be produced by dyeing.

Ticking is a tough twill weave, traditionally striped black (or blue) and white, especially made for bedding. Use it for inner covers (pillow forms) filled with feathers.

Lawn is a lightweight soft cotton available in a choice of solid colors and prints. Suitable for hand-pieced patchwork it is, however, quite fragile and not very hard-wearing.

Muslin is a medium-weight, plain-weave fabric available unbleached (natural) or bleached (white). It is inexpensive and an excellent base for dyeing and fabric painting. It is also a good choice for inner covers filled with synthetic stuffing such as polyester batting or foam.

Chintz is a closely woven cotton fabric, plain or printed, with a glazed finish that helps resist dirt and grime.

Satin is sleek with a lustrous sheen. Choose heavier weights for pillows. Silk satin is a suitable choice for silk painting. When working with slippery fabrics such as satin, place a layer of tissue paper between the two layers to be sewn.

Metallic fabrics such as those used for the Tooth Fairy pillow on page 44 and the Valentine on page 54 are not really intended for furnishings but for theatrical costumes. However, their impracticality is far outweighed by their stunning colors and textures.

Canvas is a sturdy, coarse cotton fabric used for covering deckchairs. It is quite difficult to stitch, but since it is hard-wearing, it is a good choice for outdoor cushions. Special types of canvas with an open weave and evenly spaced threads are used for needlepoint projects, such as the Farmyard Friends pillows on page 28.

Brocade is a medium or heavy satin weave with the appearance of embroidered cotton cloth. Sometimes metallic threads are included.

Moiré is a faille with a wavy watermarked effect.

Damask, first made in Damascus, is woven from silk. The elaborate weave produces a reversible pattern. Attractive but liable to crease.

Velvet is a pile cloth and can be made from cotton, silk, acetate, nylon, and other man-made fibers. It can be produced with patterns cut into the pile or with a crushed pile. Velveteen, similar to velvet, is nearly always made from cotton. When stitching velvet or other pile fabrics such as synthetic furs together, the pile should lie in the same direction. Stitch in the direction of the pile. After stitching, pull the pile out of the seam with the point of a pin.

Aftercare

After taking the trouble to make something special, it is worth looking after. Your pillows will last longer if you keep them clean and free from dust. For non-washable fabrics, instead of making removable covers, it may be easier to send the whole pillow to the cleaners.

With washable fabrics, check for shrinkage before making your cover. Wash a 4-in. (10cm) piece in hand-hot water, dry, and measure it. If it has shrunk, you will need to wash the whole piece of fabric to pre-shrink it. Wash covers regularly and if anyone spills something, act quickly: an old stain is far more difficult to remove than a fresh one. Blot excess liquids with tissue paper or a white cotton cloth. Work from the outer edge toward the middle to stop it from spreading further. Pour salt or talcum powder on dark liquids such as red wine, fruit juice, and blood to absorb moisture and some of the color. Bleach can be used on white cotton or linen, but always dilute it well, soak the whole item, not just a patch, and rinse thoroughly. Washing soda is useful for greasy stains. Mineral spirits will dissolve most paint stains.

Fillings

Whether you buy ready-made pillow forms or make your own, you have a choice of fillings. An excellent tip is to use a pad very slightly larger than your pillow cover to give a plump and very professional result.

Polyester batting is inexpensive, nonabsorbent, and washable. It is a good choice for anyone who may be allergic to feathers. One pound (0.5kg) will be enough to make a plump 18in (46cm) square pillow.

Feathers are heavy and often mixed with down. Use featherproof cambric or ticking; 2 pounds (1kg) of feathers will fill a 20-in. (50cm) pillow.

Down is expensive but very light in weight, so it is the best choice for very fine fabrics. Use downproof cambric to make the inner pad; 1 pound (0.5kg) of down will fill a 20-in. (50cm) square pillow.

Foam chippings are very inexpensive, but may prove to be a false economy as they can give a lumpy appearance and tend to crumble with age. Block foam is useful for making box cushions and can be cut to size and shape. Make an inner cover of muslin.

Kapok is sold chiefly as a filling for soft toys. This vegetable fiber is light and relatively inexpensive, but tends to become lumpy after a few years' wear. One pound (0.5kg) will fill a 15in (38cm) square pillow.

Styrofoam granules are washable, making this filling a good choice for beanbags, pet pillows, and useful for filling a neck pillow, as the granules move and mold to the shape of the body.

Buttons come in all shapes, sizes, colors, and materials. You can also buy button blanks to cover in matching or contrasting fabrics. Button fastenings can be used on any style of pillow, traditional or modern, and can be made into a feature, as in the ruffled cushion on page 22 and the colorful modern pillow on page 114.

Fastenings

The simplest pillow cover is made by stitching front to back, leaving a gap to insert the pillow form. Turn the cover right side out, put in the form, and then slip-stitch the two edges together. If you prefer to make your covers removable, however, choose a method of fastening that is appropriate to the style as well as the weight of the fabric.

Zippers

are usually concealed in a fold of fabric, in order to be as un-obtrusive as possible, but there are some colorful chunky zippers on sale which you may want to make into a feature. Generally speaking, however, invisible methods of inserting zippers are preferable, and it is usually best to insert the zipper before constructing the pillow.

To insert a zipper in a seam, baste the seam, press open, then pin, and baste the zipper in place with the teeth in line with the seam. Stitch the zipper in place, then unpick the basted seam.

To overlap a zipper, press the seam allowance in one direction, then turn back one side, leaving ¼-in. (6mm) overlap. Pin and baste the zipper in place, lining up the teeth with the narrower seam allowance. Overlap the other side to hide the zipper, pin, baste, and stitch, then stitch across the foot of the zipper.

Fastening tapes

come in two styles. Hook-and-loop fastenings consist of two tapes, one with tiny plastic hooks, the other with small loops. Popper tape holds evenly spaced metal or plastic snaps. Both of these fastening tapes have similar merits: they are washable, easy to attach by hand stitching or using a zipper foot on your machine, quick to unfasten, and very practical for pillows that will require frequent laundering. Use them in a center back opening. The disadvantage is that they are not "special" enough for a really cherished piece. Just think of them as being cheap and cheerful!

Ties can be made from strips of matching fabric, ribbons, or tapes. This method of fastening is particularly appropriate for more primitive styles of cover, but can be adapted for any style, traditional or modern. You can make a feature of ties, as in the checked contemporary cover on page 106 and the envelope slipcover on page 110.

Trimmings

Braids, cords, fringe, or lace can add just the right finishing touch to a pillow. When buying trimmings, remember to add a little extra for turning corners and joining lengths.

Trimmings can be added at the construction stage by being inserted into a seam, or they can be applied after the cover has been stitched by slip-stiching in place by hand.

Bias binding

You can buy ready-made bias binding in a multitude of solid colors and in a selection of prints. If, however, you wish to make a binding to match a particular fabric, it is easy to do. First you need to cut bias strips of fabric. To do this, find the bias grain of the fabric by folding the selvage so it lies parallel to the weft.

Cut along this edge, then mark parallel cutting lines to the width you require. Join strips together on the straight grain until you have the length you require.

To fold the edges, you can buy a special tool. Simply insert the fabric strip, pull it through, and press the folds as the strip emerges from the other side.

General Sewing

No special sewing techniques are required for making pillows, but a sewing machine is a useful tool. Zigzag stitch can be used to hold appliqué shapes in place, and machine buttonholes make attractive fastenings.

Corners
After stitching, clip corners by cutting straight across, close to corner seam.

Boxed corners
Stitch up to the corner, cut out a small square of fabric at the corner point, then continue to stitch down the other side. Reinforce by stitching a second line on top of the first.

Curves
For an inside or an outside curve, clip notches in the seam allowance right up to the stitching line.

Ruffles
Before gathering, mark the ruffle into sections, corresponding to the points on the pillow cover where it is to be attached. (For example, for a square pillow, mark four equal sections to correspond with the center point of each side.) Gather each section in turn and pull up to fit. Pin, baste, and then stitch in place.

Sewing machine

with a swing needle for zigzag and buttonhole stitches.

Paper and cardboard – for

patchwork templates, use scrap paper.

Equipment

The items on this page make up the basic equipment needed to produce all the projects in this book.

Needles – crewel for

embroidery, tapestry for needlepoint and cross stitch, sharps for general hand sewing

Pins – fine stainless

steel for general use and glass-headed for patchwork and quilting.

Embroidery scissors for snipping

threads, clipping seams and cutting notches.

Paintbrushes –

a selection of good quality artists' brushes for applying fabric paint.

Rotary cutter for

cutting several layers of fabric simultaneously, indispensable for accurate cutting of patchwork pieces.

Large stretcher frame for fabric painting.

Tjanting for applying wax

in batik painting.

Embroidery hoop

for stretching fabric when embroidering.

Dressmaking shears – good quality and

very sharp.

Cutting mat

Tape measure

Ruler

Paper scissors good

quality and very sharp.

Country

If your heart is in the country then faded florals, frills and flounces, simple stripes, buttons, and bows will contribute the perfect touch of homeliness to your humble abode. These pillows are casual, simple, and very pretty, owing much to providence and the thrifty hoarding of scraps. Traditional crafts are skills to treasure and even in the hustle and bustle of the modern world, patchwork and appliqué still fulfil an important recycling role.

Chair Cushion

In pretty cotton prints, this seat cushion and matching chair back is a classic way to decorate plain kitchen chairs.

Make your kitchen a cozy, comforting place with these pretty chair covers. Fashioned from pretty prints in colors to coordinate with the paintwork, the easy-to-make cushions cover and protect hard seats and are held in place with matching ties.

To make covers to fit your own chairs, you need to make a paper pattern. This is used to cut the fabric and batting, and you then just add a strip for the ruffle.

1 Cut a paper pattern from tracing paper or newspaper. Lay the paper on the seat and trace around the seat edge with a pencil. To be sure of a symmetrical shape, fold the paper in half, from back to front, then cut around the outline.

2 Using this paper pattern as your template and adding $^1/_2$-in. (13mm) seam allowance all around, cut out two seat pieces from the large-print fabric. Using the same paper pattern but without adding seam allowance, cut out three or four pieces of batting.

3 To make the pleated ruffle, measure the front and sides of your template. Add all three measurements together and double the total. Now cut a piece of contrasting fabric measuring this length by 13in. (33cm) wide. It may be necessary to join fabric pieces to obtain the desired length.

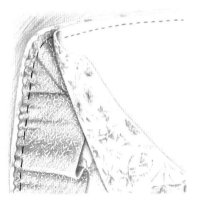

4 Fold the ruffle in half lengthwise and gather or pleat the raw edges. Pin and baste this ruffle in place on the right side of one of the cushion pieces. Place the other cushion piece on it right sides together and stitch around the sides and front,

leaving the back open. Clip corners and curves, and turn right side out. Insert batting.

5 Cut four ties from the whole width of the larger print fabric, each measuring 3in. (7.5cm) across. Fold in half lengthwise, right sides together, and stitch with a $^1/_2$-in. (13mm) seam, leaving one end open. Turn right side out and press.

6 Slipstitch the opening on the cushion cover, inserting the ties as you work and stitching them firmly in place.

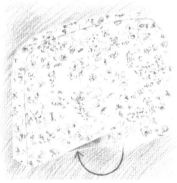

7 To make the slipcover for the chair back, measure the width of the chair and decide on the depth you wish the cover to be. Cut out two pieces of both fabric and lining to these dimensions, one each for the back and front, adding $^1/_2$-in. (13mm) seam allowance. Measure the top edge

Materials

* $^3/_4$yd (0.7m) of 48in. (122cm) cotton fabric, in large floral print

* $^1/_2$yd (0.45m) of 48in. (122cm) cotton fabric, in coordinating small floral print

* $^1/_2$yd (0.45m) of 48in. (122cm) plain cotton lining fabric

* $^1/_2$yd (0.45m) of 48in. (122cm) medium-weight polyester batting

* sewing thread to match fabric

and two sides, add these measurements together, and cut out a gusset from the same fabric and lining, making it $2^1/_2$in. (6cm) wide (or the width of your chair plus a double seam allowance). Join the gusset to both back and front pieces; do the same with the lining. Cut a piece of batting to fit inside the casing and place it inside the slipcover. Slip the lining inside, turn under raw edges, and slipstitch together.

Tips
Depending on the shape of your chair back, you may need to leave an opening in one of the side seams of the slipcover for it to be put in place. Add a button or hook-and-loop fastening to the bottom of this opening.

Buttons and Frills

Make a feature of your fastenings – button up a pretty pastel pillow with a hand crocheted trim.

This pillow feels as soft as it looks. The crocheted lace gives a cozy, old-fashioned feel and actually acts as the fastening: tiny pearl buttons slip neatly into the picot edging, making it practical as well as pretty. The crochet pattern is an easy one, even for relative beginners. Of course, you could adapt your own favorite edging pattern, aiming to make a piece approximately 3in. (7.5cm) wide by 10–11in. (25–27cm) in length and incorporating chain loops to serve as buttonholes.

The fabric is a warm wool and cotton check in pastel shades of blue and white, and pink and white – scraps left over from making cozy pajamas for my children.

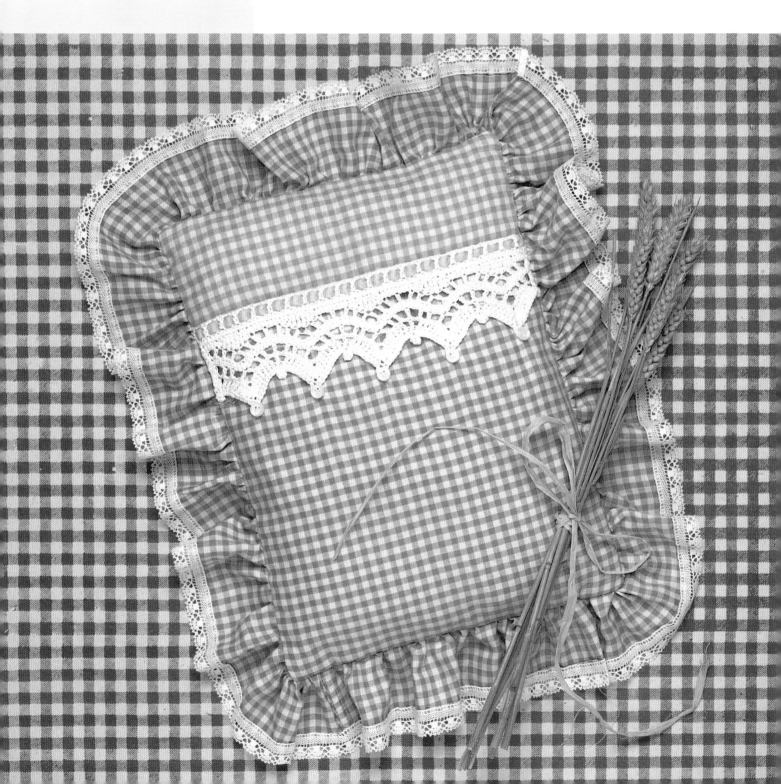

1 To make the crochet lace, make a foundation chain of 85 stitches; turn. Row 1: make 3 chains, * skip 1, then make one (double crochet) treble into the next chain; continue from * to end; turn. Row 2: make 2 chains, then work one row of single crochet (double crochet); turn. Now work from the chart on page 118. To make the buttonholes, work a row of single crochet (double crochet) along the top edge of the lace, making picots (a loop of 4 chains) in the center of each dip and point.

2 Thread ribbon through the eyelet edging of the crochet lace. Hem one long edge of the pink fabric and stitch lace in place on top.

3 Cut a rectangle from the blue fabric, measuring 11 × 12in. (27 × 30cm). Hem one of the longer edges. Place the pink fabric piece over the blue one, with the lace overlapping the hemmed edge of the blue fabric. Mark positions for buttons and stitch in place. Fasten buttons.

4 Cut the pillow back from the blue fabric, measuring 12 × 15in. (30 × 38cm). From the remaining blue fabric, cut a ruffle measuring 3in. (7.5cm) wide and 54in. (137cm) long, joining fabric strips where necessary to obtain this length.

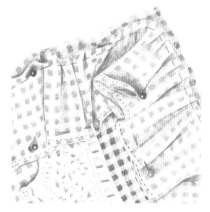

5 Hem one long edge of the fabric strip and gather the other edge. Join short ends. Pull up gathering so the ruffle fits around the pillow. Pin and baste to pillow front.

6 Place pillow back on top, right sides facing, and stitch all around with a ½-in. (13mm) seam allowance. Undo buttons and turn right side out through opening. Insert pillow form and fasten buttons.

Materials

* ½yd (45cm) of 36-in. (90cm) wide blue and white checked fabric
* 5 × 12-in. (12 × 30cm) remnant of pink and white checked fabric
* 1 × 1-oz (25g) ball of crochet cotton no. 6, in white
* 1.75mm crochet hook
* 12-in. (30cm) length of ¼-in. (6mm) ribbon, in pale blue
* 5 × ⅜in. (1cm) white buttons
* matching sewing thread
* 12 × 15-in. (30 × 38cm) pillow form

Tips

To make sure the ruffle does not get caught in the seams, pin or baste it toward the center, out of the way while you are stitching, then remove pins or basting once you have turned the cover right side out.

Heart Appliqué

Turn dressmaking scraps into a pillow to cherish – homespun hearts on a plump pillow with a cheery checked ruffle.

Here's another good excuse to raid your rag bag and sort your scraps. This pretty pillow has a cozy quality because it has been made from dressmaking scraps. The only formal part of the pattern is in alternating solid and patterned pieces. Other than that, the only thing that links things is family memories – a piece of a summer pinafore, a picnic cloth, a pillowcase, and a school shirt – preserved in a plump pillow.

This project combines the techniques of patchwork, appliqué, and quilting. The background squares are pieced by hand or machine, the hearts applied with deft handstitching, and the whole enhanced by neat rows of running stitch.

1 Use ¼-in. (6mm) seams throughout. Cut 12 squares of 4in. (10cm), six solid and six patterned. Join the square patches, by hand or machine, in three rows of four, alternating solid and patterned fabrics.

2 Cut out 12 hearts, using the template on page 120 as a guide. Turn under raw edges of heart shapes, pin and baste in place. Stitch to background patchwork, using small, neat stitches. (For tips on appliqué technique, see page 103.)

3 Using different colored embroidery threads with two strands in the needle, work rows of running stitches all around hearts and edges of patches.

4 Stitch buttons securely at the intersections of patches.

5 Make the ruffle. Cut the checked fabric lengthwise into four strips of equal width, then join to form one continuous strip. Hem one long edge with a narrow double hem, then run a double row of gathering stitches along the other edge. Repeat with the other fabrics.

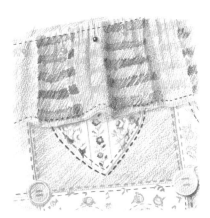

6 Pull up gathering thread on each ruffle piece to fit around the pillow. Pin, baste, and stitch the three ruffles together through all thicknesses of fabric.

7 Pin the triple ruffle to the right side of the pillow front as shown, allowing extra gathers at corners. Baste in place.

Materials

* scraps of printed, checked, and solid cotton fabrics

* 12 × 16in. (30 × 40cm) remnant of cotton fabric, for backing

* 10in. (25cm) of 36-in. (90cm) checked fabric for outer ruffle

* 8in. (20cm) of 36-in. (90cm) printed fabric for middle ruffle

* 4in. (10cm) of 36-in. (90cm) gingham fabric for inner ruffle

* assorted lengths of 6-stranded embroidery thread

* crewel needle

* 6 buttons

* matching sewing thread

* 11 × 15-in. (28 × 38cm) pillow form

8 Assemble the pillow cover. With right sides together, stitch front to back along three sides, with a ½-in. (13mm) seam allowance, making sure you do not catch ruffle in seam, and leaving a gap for turning. Clip corners, turn right side out, insert pillow form, and close opening.

Homespun Heart

An appliqué heart adds a touch of individuality to a simple little pillow.

When you want to make something special but you just haven't got the time, choose a colorful fabric that speaks for itself, like this lively mixture of woven checks and stripes. Then add just a little embellishment, such as a simple heart.

This particular fabric lends itself so well to a plain, square cover. Pieces have been carefully cut so that the gingham squares form the four corners of the cover, and the striped squares form a cross with a plain square right in the center. Two heart shapes, one slightly smaller than the other, have been cut from other parts of the cloth, and machined in place, using a close zigzag stitch.

Materials

* 16in. of 54in.- (40cm of 140cm) medium-weight woven check fabric

* scraps of cotton fabric in plain red and contrasting pattern

* matching sewing thread

* 12in. (30cm) square pillow form

1 Cut two squares of check fabric, each measuring 1¼in. (3cm). From scraps of fabric, cut two heart shapes, one in plain red fabric approximately 2½in. (6cm) wide, and the other in a contrasting pattern about 3½in. (8cm) wide.

3 With right sides facing, place the two halves of the cover together and stitch along three sides. Clip corners and turn right side out. Insert pillow form and close opening.

2 Place the larger heart in the center of the front cover, pin in position, then stitch by machine, using a close zigzag stitch, or by hand using satin stitch. Place the smaller heart in the center of the first heart and stitch in place.

Variations

Instead of a heart, cut any simple shape you like – a flower, fish, duck, leaf, or star would all look equally effective.

Farmyard Friends

This pair of little pillows features a chicken and duck in needlepoint with a patchwork effect.

Small-scale needlepoint panels are quick to stitch and very effective when given a cheery border of multicolored dots. The needlepoint design has a patchwork effect, with stripes, checks, and dots. Then a border of dotted fabric in various color combinations has been added to create a pair of pillows that would look right at home on a rocking chair in the kitchen, or in a child's room.

The panels have been worked in tent stitch, which creates a firm, hard wearing fabric. The amounts given in the list of materials are for both pillows. If you have any scraps of tapestry yarn in your work basket, this is an ideal project for using them up.

1 Stretch the canvas on a frame. Using a single strand of tapestry yarn in your needle, work the two designs, side by side, allowing 2in. (5cm) of space between them. Following the chart on page 30, and using the photograph of the finished pillows as a guide, work the designs in tent stitch. One colored square on the chart represents a single tent stitch worked across one intersection of canvas threads.

2 When the designs have been stitched, remove the canvas from the frame and cut them out, leaving a border of approximately 1in. (2.5cm) around each design.

3 Stitch the pieces of dotted fabric to the canvas, by hand or machine, with right sides together and seams close to the edge of the needlepoint so that no unworked canvas will show on the finished pillow.

4 Position the fabric pieces so that they begin at one corner of the needlepoint and join the next colored piece to form a stepped border. Trim off excess fabric to form a square pillow front measuring approximately 13in. (33cm).

5 With right sides together, stitch front of pillow to back, leaving a gap for turning. Insert a zipper in opening. Turn right side out and insert pillow form.

Materials

* *tapestry yarn, one skein of each of the following: jade green, yellow, pale blue, purple, sugar pink, turquoise, coffee, royal blue, bright pink, lavender, blue, sand, scarlet, pale gray, tan, terracotta, white, and black

* *8 × 14in. (20 × 35cm) 10-gauge canvas

* *8 pieces of dotted fabric, each measuring approximately 5 × 9in. (12.5 × 23cm)

* *2 pieces of backing fabric, each 13in. (33cm) square

* *2 pieces of 11-in. (28cm) square pillow forms

Variations

Why not make a rectangular pillow featuring both birds? Simply join the two charts together and stitch the hen and duck either facing each other, or back to back. By adding a border 4¹/₂in. (11.5cm) wide (as on the square pillows), you will end up with a pillow of 11 × 16in. (28 × 40cm).

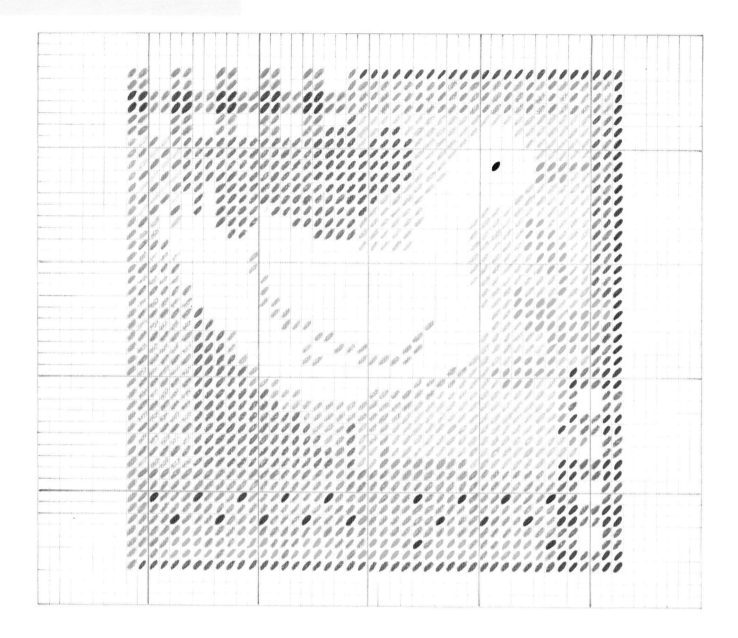

	DMC no.	Color		DMC no.	Color		DMC no.	Color
	7957	jade green		7807	turquoise		7503	sand
	7786	yellow		7846	coffee		7606	scarlet
		black		7797	royal blue		7300	pale gray
	7298	palest blue		7602	bright pink		7445	tan
	7242	purple		7711	lavender		7439	terracotta
	7605	sugar pink		7283	pale blue			white

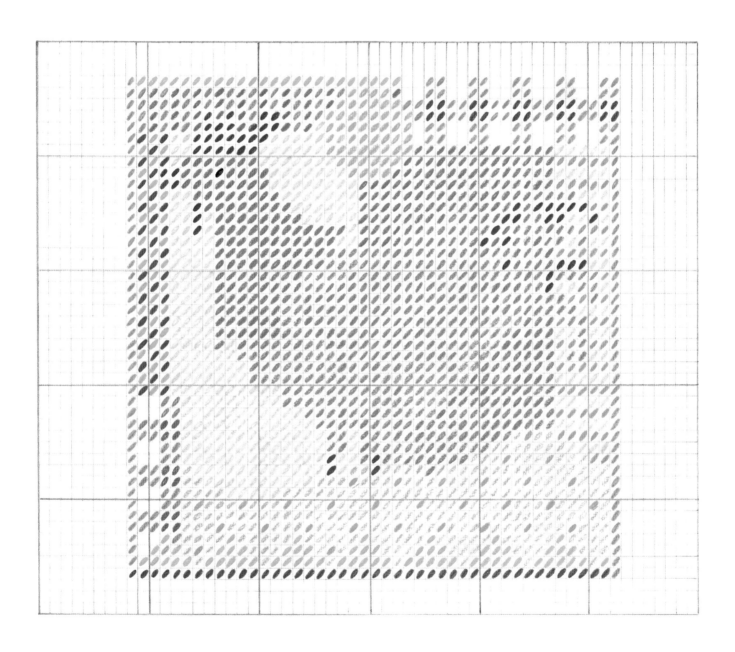

Pretty Patchwork

Use this pillow to soften the seat of a favorite garden chair – and stir fond memories.

The charm of this pillow lies in the array of different fabrics. These are literally scraps! Tiny pieces of fabric left over from other projects or rescued from my children's outgrown summer dresses are never discarded but hoarded in a basket. Now a handful of them have been transformed into a pretty patchwork – a memory pillow.

Made from hand-pieced patches, this pillow is practical as well as pretty, as it is made like a quilt, with a layer of batting, and can be easily laundered. Use it on the seat of a garden chair, kitchen chair, or stool. Add ties, if you like, plus a few buttons and a froth of lace, then sit back with your thoughts and memories.

1 Trace the diamond-shaped template from page 118 on thick paper and cut out 114 paper patches.

2 Now cut out the same number of fabric patches, ¼in. (6mm) larger all around than the papers.

3 Make the patches by placing a paper in the center of the wrong side of a fabric patch and turning the raw edges of the fabric over. Baste, taking your needle right through the fabric and paper.

4 Join patches by placing right sides together and overcast edges with small, neat stitches. Join the diamond shapes in rows, using the photograph as a guide.

5 To assemble the pillow, place three layers of batting between the patchwork and backing fabrics with their right sides out. Baste all around, close to the raw edges, through all thicknesses of fabric and batting. Trim edges.

6 Quilt the pillow by stitching rows of running stitches through all thicknesses and following the contours of the patches. Stitch several rows of quilting in this way, adding buttons as you go to add surface interest and to hold the batting firmly in place.

7 Bind the raw edges with bias binding. Stitch the lace on top of the binding, on the under-side of the pillow (see photograph).

8 If you wish to add ties to secure the pillow to a chair, cut the ribbon in two equal lengths, fold each piece in half and attach to the underside of the pillow, close to the two back corners.

Variations

If you want a more formal effect, you could work each row of patches in a single print, for stripes, or you could use just two or three fabrics.

Materials

* scraps of cotton dress-weight fabrics

* 16 × 16in. (40 × 40cm) plain or printed cotton fabric, for backing

* 1⅝yd (1.5m) of 1-in. (2.5cm) pale blue bias binding

* sewing thread, in cream, pale blue, and pink

* ½yd (0.4m) lightweight batting

* 4 buttons

* 1⅝yd (1.5m) of 1¾-in. (4cm) wide gathered cotton lace

* 2yd (1.8m) of ½-in. (13mm) wide ribbon (optional)

Tips

Use pure cotton fabrics instead of blends for patchwork, as the fabric creases better, giving a crisp edge, and is easier to stitch. Use cotton thread for sewing. It is not necessary to match the color of the thread to the different-colored fabrics – just choose a neutral shade, such as cream, white, or pale blue, and make sure your stitches are small and neat.

Postage Stamp Patchwork

This is a jolly little pillow with its bright assortment of colored patches and cheerful checked ruffle.

It is easy to see where this cushion gets its name. The bright patchwork pieces are about the same size as the average postage stamp and just as colorful. With hardly two pieces the same, here is a chance to use up the tiniest scraps from your work basket to good effect. The only formal element to this random arrangement is that plain and patterned patches have been alternated throughout.

Just the right size for a footstool, this cushion would also be charming on a child's chair.

1 Cut 63 paper patches, each measuring 1 × 1¼in. (30 × 25mm) (see Tips).

2 Cut rectangles of fabric approximately ¼in. (6mm) larger all around than the paper patches. Place a paper patch on the wrong side of a fabric piece, fold fabric edges over, and baste in place. Repeat until you have 63 patches.

3 To join the patches, place two right sides together with edges level, and overcast edges with small, neat stitches. Make seven rows, each with nine patches.

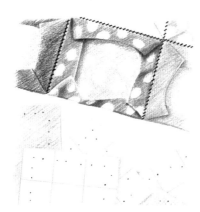

4 When all the patches are joined together, remove basting stitches and papers and press.

5 Place patchwork and backing fabric right sides together, and stitch around three sides, with a ¼-in. (6mm) seam. Clip corners, turn the cover right side out, and press lightly.

6 Pin and baste gathered ruffle to back of cover, easing in fullness at corners. Insert the pillow form and close the gap with small, neat stitches.

Materials

*scraps of cotton fabric in various colors and patterns, 63 pieces each at least 1¾ × 2in. (45 × 50mm)

*8 × 12in. (21 × 30cm) cotton fabric for backing

*4⅝yd (4.25m) of 2-in. (5cm) gathered trimming (see Tips)

*sewing thread to match backing fabric and trimming

*7 × 10-in. (27 × 17.5cm) pillow form

Tips

A pre-gathered cotton trimming has been added after the cushion cover has been made up. If you prefer, you can make a fabric frill and insert it between the back and front pieces of the cover, following the instructions for gathered ruffles on page 16.

*

This patchwork has been hand-pieced using paper patches, following the same method as described for the Pretty Patchwork seat cushion on page 32. If you prefer, you could stitch the pieces using a sewing machine.

Exotic

Sumptuous velvet, beautiful brocade, slippery silks and satins are the fabrics of the theater, and the harem! Opulence and indulgence are the operative words. Stimulate your senses with materials that are not only beautiful to look at but tactile, too. Indulge your sense of drama with colors that shimmer. The pillows in this chapter are also for sharing, with some stunning ideas for glitzy gifts.

Leopard Print

Go wild with needle and yarn, and create this opulent little pillow with a needlepoint panel and black velvet border.

You can be king of the jungle with this fabulous *trompe l'oeil* pillow. The look of leopard skin is easily conjured up with a few skeins of tapestry yarn and a bit of nimble stitching.

To make a hard-wearing fabric, the needlepoint has been stitched in tent stitch – but work it in half cross stitch if you prefer and you will need about 30 percent less yarn than the amounts given.

As a finishing touch, this pillow has been edged with rope braid, but you could add a silky fringe or faux-fur trimming if you prefer.

1 Stretch the canvas on a frame. Using a single strand of tapestry yarn in your needle, work the design, following the chart on page 119. One colored square on the chart represents a single tent stitch worked across one intersection of canvas threads.

2 When the whole design has been stitched, remove the work from the frame. Trim the canvas all around to make a border of approximately 1in. (2.5cm).

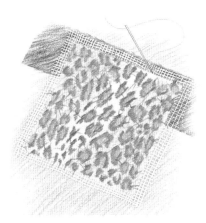

3 Cut four strips of velvet, each measuring 3¹/₂ × 15in. (9 × 38cm). Stitch these strips to canvas by hand or machine, with seams

close to edge of needlepoint so that no unworked canvas will show on the finished pillow.

4 Join velvet strips, mitering corners. Cut a pillow back measuring 15 × 15in. (38 × 38cm) from velvet. With right sides together, stitch front to back, leaving a gap for turning. Then insert zipper in opening. Turn right side out, insert pillow form, and close opening.

5 Add trimming, catching it to seam with small stitches. Twist cord into a loop at each corner. Hide ends of cord in seam.

Materials

- *11 × 11-in. (28 × 28cm) square of 10-gauge canvas

- *tapestry yarn in the following amounts and colors: 5 skeins butter, 2 skeins honey, 2 skeins cream, 3 skeins bitter chocolate, 3 skeins chocolate, 2 skeins cappuccino

- *15 × 19in. (38 × 48cm) black velvet

- *matching sewing thread

- *14 × 14-in. (35 × 35cm) pillow form

- *lightweight zipper (optional)

- *2¼yd (2m) brown cord, for trimming

Tips

It is easier to work needlepoint on a frame and has the advantage of keeping the canvas taut so it is less liable to distort as you stitch. If, however, the finished work is not square, dampen the canvas and pin the work on a board, pulling it into shape. Pin it all around with thumbtacks and leave for a few days until completely dry, before making the pillow.

Star-stamped Ball

If you like star-gazing, you'll love this planet-shaped pillow subtly stamped with golden stars.

Stamping is a simple and popular decorative technique that can be easily adapted to fabric printing. Just use a fabric paint in a subtle shade of gold and stamp your motif on the fabric of your choice.

Here the fine ribbed texture of glossy black faille breaks up the surface of the paint to create a soft effect. Choose a slinky panne velvet, a slippery satin, or smooth cotton chintz, and you will achieve different effects. Experiment on scraps before you commit yourself to a larger quantity of fabric.

The sphere-shaped pillow is a novelty item that can be adapted to different furnishing styles. The most obvious is in the playroom, where each segment could be cut from a different colored fabric to produce a

multicolored ball. A more stylish treatment, however, could be to include this globe shape in an assortment of pillows of different shapes and sizes, all covered in the same fabric – such as a soft shade of velvet.

Materials

* ½yd (45cm) of 48-in. (122cm) wide plain black fabric, for cover

* ½yd (45cm) of 36-in. (90cm) wide cotton cambric or ticking, for pillow form

* synthetic filling

* star-shaped rubber stamp

* fabric paint, in gold

* small paint roller (optional)

* fine paintbrush

* black sewing thread

* 2 gold tassels

1 Photocopy the pattern on page 125, enlarging it to the size you want. This pillow was made from segments 18in. (46cm) in length, including a ⅜-in. (1cm) seam allowance.

2 Using the template as a cutting guide, cut eight segments from black fabric and eight from cambric or ticking.

4 Print each segment of black fabric with a random pattern of stars, applying the paint to the rubber stamp with a roller or brush. If you wish, you can touch up areas of the stamped stars using the paintbrush dipped in gold fabric paint.

5 Assemble the cover in the same way as the pillow form. Insert the form into the opening and close with neat hand stitching.

6 Finish the ends, where all the segments meet, by stitching tassels in place.

3 Make the pillow form first. With right sides facing, stitch segments together, leaving an opening in the final seam for turning. Clip curves and turn right side out. Stuff firmly with synthetic filling and close the opening by hand stitching.

Tips
Choose a firm fabric for this pillow, one that will hold its shape. You can vary the size of the pillow according to how large you blow up the pattern on the photocopier.

Tooth Fairy

A shimmering shooting star, this tiny pillow, made from sparkly metallic fabrics, holds a special secret.

When you wish upon a star…the tooth fairy might just come while you are asleep and leave a shiny coin in the pocket of this little pillow, in exchange for a baby tooth. What child could resist such a special little pillow?

Metallic lamé, though it looks extravagant, is relatively inexpensive. You will need only a small remnant to make the star-shaped pillow, and an even smaller scrap for the pocket. The silver star in the center was bought in a craft store, but you could make one using your own paper pattern, or substitute a button or sequin.

Add the finishing flourish with a rainbow trail of space-dyed ribbon streamers; then wrap up the whole package as a gift for your favorite small person.

Materials

*2 scraps of gold lamé, each measuring 12 × 12in. (30 × 30cm)

*scrap of pink metallic fabric, 3½ × 9½in. (9 × 24cm)

*13-in. (33cm) length of ¾-in. (2cm) single satin ribbon, in pink

*sewing thread, in pink

*synthetic filling

*1 snap fastener

*1 star-shaped patch, button, sequin, or other ornament

*1½yd (1.4m) of 1½-in. (39mm) sheer ribbon, in Sunbeam

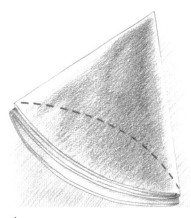

1 To make a pattern for the pillow, fold a circle of paper, 12in. (30cm) in diameter, into six segments, then cut a curved shape from the lower edge. Use this template to cut two star shapes from the gold lamé fabric.

3 At the point of the flap, stitch one half of the snap to the underside, and the other half to the center of the pocket. Cut the sheer ribbon into five pieces of varying lengths and sew to the flap. Stitch the star-shaped ornament on top to hide the ribbon ends.

2 Cut one end of the pink metallic fabric to a point, to form the flap of the pocket. Bind the opposite straight end with a piece of pink ribbon. Fold up a third of the fabric, to make a pocket, and use the remaining ribbon to bind the raw edges.

4 Stitch the front and back pieces of the pillow cover together, right sides facing, with a ½-in. (13mm) seam. Leave a gap for turning. Clip corners and curves and turn right side out. Stuff fairly firmly with synthetic filling, pushing it into the points of the star. Stitch opening closed.

Tips

If the fabric you choose is very flimsy, strengthen it by backing it with iron-on interfacing.

Turkish Delight

Perfect for lounging in palatial comfort, this extravagant bolster takes only minutes to put together.

Choose a rich upholstery fabric reminiscent of a Turkish carpet with jewel-like colors, for this sumptuous bolster cushion.

This really is a low-sew project, with only one seam to stitch. There is no need to hem the ends as they are tucked in and held in place with a cord tied tightly around. Choose a luxurious tasseled cord or make one yourself following the instructions on page 80.

Materials

*⅞yd (80cm) of 54-in. (140cm) wide upholstery fabric

*matching sewing thread

*bolster pad, 18in. (45cm) long, 7in. (18cm) diameter

*2 tasseled cords

1 Cut a piece of fabric wide enough to go around the bolster pad with 2 to 3in. (5 to 7.5cm) to spare – about 26in. (66cm).

2 Form the fabric into a long tube and stitch a seam 1¼in. (3cm) from the long edges.

3 Push the bolster pad into the center of the tube. Fold in selvages to meet the end of the bolster, then tie a tasseled cord around each end close to the ends of the pad.

Tips

Buy a bolster pad or make your own. Alternatively, roll up a rug or towel into a tight cylindrical shape.

Japanese Silk Painting

Paint an exotic oriental-style picture in beautiful bright colors on smooth, sensuous silk.

A colorful painting on fine silk makes a pillow to display proudly on a favorite chair. For a decorative flourish, add splashes of bright ribbon at the corners, weighted with beads in natural wood.

The technique used to create the picture on this cover is the same as for the spotted pillow on page 100, though the finished result is quite different. You first paint the outline design with water-based gutta used straight from the tube. Then fill in the shapes with color using silk paints.

You will need to stretch the fabric – plain, inexpensive silk habutai – on a frame, but once you have done that, painting is very simple.

1 Mark a 16-in. (40cm) square in the center of the silk fabric, using a water-erasable pen. Within this, mark the design, tracing the fish from page 119 and drawing the rest freehand, using the photograph of the finished pillow as a guide. If you make a mistake or want to change part of the drawing, simply redraw as the marks will fade when dampened.

2 Stretch the fabric on a frame, securing it with masking tape. Paint over the design you have drawn, using black gutta for the main parts of the design and pearl white for clouds, ripples in the stream, and to highlight the fish's scales. Make sure that the gutta sinks into the fibers of the fabric and that there are no breaks in the lines.

3 Fill in the pattern with silk paints used straight from the bottle for the sky, water, fish, flowers, and leaves. Mix shades of brown from green, blue, yellow, and raspberry to paint the mountains and earth. There is no need to let each color dry before beginning the next, as the gutta lines will prevent paints from running into each other.

4 Leave to dry for several hours. Then remove fabric from frame and set colors by ironing on the reverse of the fabric for at least 3–4 minutes.

5 Leave for 2–3 days. Then wash fabric to remove gutta residue and leave to dry.

6 Press the fabric to remove creases and trim the painted panel to a square measuring 15$\frac{1}{2}$in. (39cm). With right sides together, stitch front to back with a $\frac{1}{2}$-in. (13mm) seam, leaving a gap to insert pillow form. Close the gap with small, neat stitches.

7 To decorate the corners, cut the ribbon into 6-in. (15cm) lengths. Attach four lengths of ribbon to each corner with several stitches to hold them firmly in place. Add a large wooden bead, held in place with a small flat wooden bead and a tiny glass bead.

Materials

- *20-in. (50cm) square of white silk habutai

- *water-erasable pen

- *colorless gutta, one tube each of black and pearl white

- *silk paints, one 1½-oz (45ml) bottle of each of the following colors: primary yellow, mandarin yellow, raspberry pink, bright blue, azure blue, green, salmon

- *20-in. (50cm) square of yellow silk habutai, for backing

- *matching sewing thread

- *15-in. (38cm) square pillow form

- *3yd (2.75m) of ¼-in. (6mm) double-faced satin ribbon in yellow gold

- *4 large wooden beads, 4 small flat wooden beads, and 4 glass seed beads

Tips

The finished pillow measures 14½in. (37cm) square and is filled with a 15-in. (38cm) pillow form. By making the cover slightly smaller than the pad, the fabric is stretched, displaying the painting to its best advantage.

Floral Fantasy

Choose bright colors for maximum impact and the technique of machine appliqué for speed, to create a fantastic floral concoction.

Contemporary methods of creative stitchery can allow you to be very inventive. With a sewing machine, assorted fabric scraps, and a brave sense of color, you can conjure up a designer original in next to no time. No special techniques are used; everything is held in place with machine stitching.

This style would fit in well with modern furnishings, and you can choose your own palette of colors – just make them nice and bright! The square patches on this pillow – silks, plain cottons, and chintzes – are vivid red, emerald, tangerine, fuchsia pink, sunshine yellow, and Granny Smith green, next to slightly more subdued shades of ice blue, cornflower, primrose, dusty pink, and claret. What brings these disparate colors together

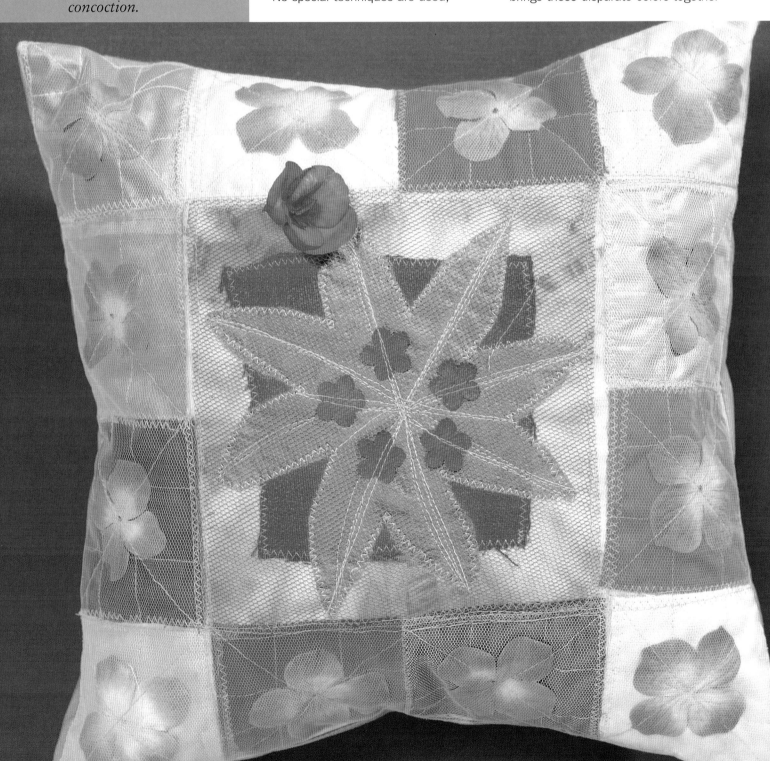

are the machine stitching and a gauzy overlay of nylon net. The background fabric is cotton, tie-dyed in peachy shades; and though it is hardly visible, glimpsed only through the gaps, its subtle shading does contribute to the overall effect. Trapped between the layers are the petals of artificial flowers. These are cut from a hydrangea, but you could use any flowers that have an interesting formation of petals and which can be pressed flat.

1 Cut the fabric scraps into 16 3½-in. (9cm) squares. Arrange them to form a border. Move them around until you are pleased with the arrangement, then stitch around the edge of each square using a medium zigzag stitch.

2 Cut a larger square, measuring approximately 5 × 5in. (12.5 × 12.5cm) and place it in the center. Stitch it in place with zigzag stitching. Cut a large, star-like flower shape from a contrasting color and stitch on top.

3 Place a flower on each square and several in the center, lay a square of tulle or net on top, and hold in place with pins. Machine stitch, using a straight stitch and a different colored thread.

4 Trim the pillow front to measure the same as the back, then stitch the two pieces together, right sides facing. Leave an opening in one side, clip corners, and turn right side out. Insert the pillow form and close opening by hand stitching.

Materials

* *16 × 16in. (40 × 40cm) plain or subtly patterned fabric, for pillow front

* *15 × 15in. (38 × 38cm) plain, brightly colored fabric, for pillow back

* *scraps of bright solid-colored fabrics

* *scraps of tulle and bridal veiling

* *sewing thread, in two or more colors

* *fabric flowers

* *15-in. (38cm) square pillow form

Tips
The use of artificial flowers and assorted fabrics means that this cover cannot be washed, so it is not suitable for heavy wear. It could, however, be dry-cleaned – so dispense with any fastenings and take the whole pillow, not just the cover, to the cleaner.

Velvet Stars

Scintillating stars adorn a plush velvet bolster to bring a touch of exotica to your boudoir.

If practicality is not a priority, and pure luxury is your aim, then a velvet bolster shot through with shining stars is sure to appeal.

Astonishingly simple to put together, this cover is compiled from inexpensive upholstery velvet decorated with machine-appliqué stars cut from a more luxurious panné velvet. The addition of fake gems is an unashamed indulgence. Leave them off, if you wish, or replace with buttons or with shapes of the same or a contrasting velvet.

1 Trace the star motif from page 118 directly onto the paper backing of the fusible bonding web with a pencil. Trace eight motifs in all, then cut them out roughly, leaving a small margin around each shape.

2 Using a hot, dry iron, fuse the pieces of bonding web to the wrong side of the panné velvet, following the manufacturer's instructions.

3 Cut out the velvet shapes along the pencil lines. Then peel off the backing paper.

4 Cut the green velvet fabric to a rectangle measuring 23 × 26in. (58 × 66cm). Arrange the stars on this fabric, keeping a margin of approximately 4in. (10cm) clear at each end. Fuse the stars onto the backing fabric with a hot iron.

5 Thread your sewing machine needle with gold embroidery thread and the bobbin with dark blue. Using a medium zigzag stitch and loose tension, stitch around the outlines of the star shapes.

6 Stitch the fake gems in place by hand, using dark blue thread.

7 Join the two longer ends of the fabric with a ¹/₂-in. (1cm) seam. Turn right side out and insert the bolster form. Run a gathering thread through each of the two ends of the cover and pull up tightly. Tuck in raw edges.

8 Cut the piece of ribbon into two equal lengths. Run a gathering thread close to one edge. Join the two ends of the ribbon, then pull up to make a rosette. Stitch the rosettes in place

at each end of the bolster to cover the openings. Stitch the tassels and the remaining fake jewels in place on top.

Materials

- *23 × 26in. (58 × 66cm) upholstery-weight velvet in sea green
- *remnant of panné velvet in midnight blue
- *fusible bonding web
- *10 fake sapphires, approximately 1in. (2.5cm) diameter
- *machine embroidery thread in light gold
- *dark blue and sea green sewing thread
- *bolster form, 18in. (45cm) long, 7in. (18cm) diameter
- *½yd (0.45m) of 1-in. (0.45m) wide ribbon in green/lilac
- *2 gold tassels

Tips

If you wish, instead of machine stitching, decorate the edges of the stars with hand stitching, either satin stitch or blanket stitch, using the same metallic thread.

Vibrant Valentine

Romantic red and passionate pink fabrics make a startling statement in this unconventional love token.

If you want to make a pillow for your love – make it heart-shaped! Combine fabrics of different textures, choose colors that positively scream, then add faux jewels, trinkets, and even a picture of the object of your desire. Round it off with trashy trim, such as this cotton bobble trimming which has been dyed peach using cold water dye, and you have a dream of a pillow – or the ultimate in kitsch, depending on personal taste.

The foundation fabric is a bright red cotton, the central heart is orange lamé edged with sequins, the border is from an old sari shot with gold thread, and seams are hidden with a narrow satin ribbon in turquoise. Jewels and charms make laundering impossible, but practicality cannot always be the priority!

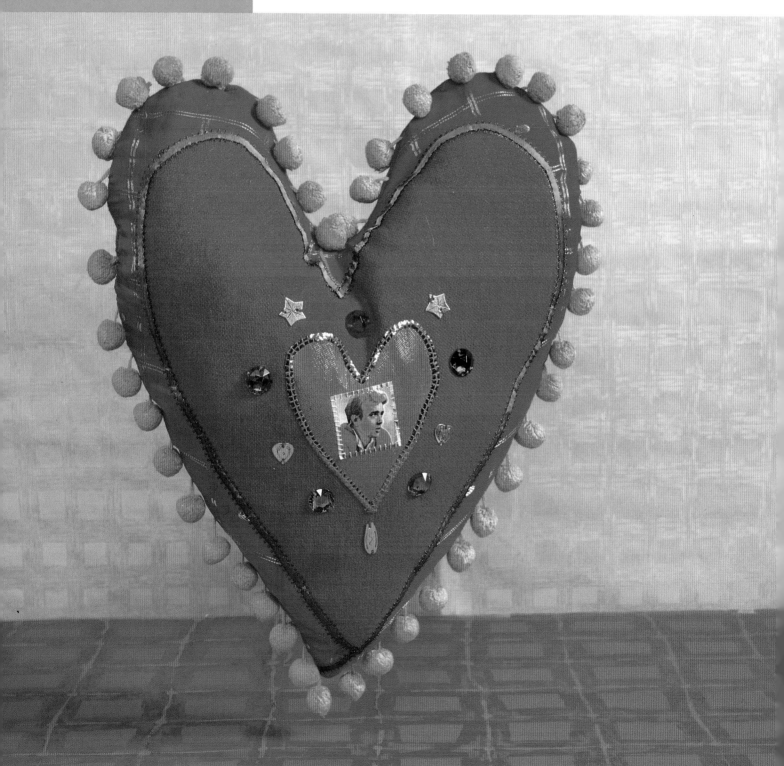

1 Cut two heart shapes from red fabric, using the template on page 120 enlarged to a width of 12in. (30cm). Cut a 1-in. (2.5cm) border from pink fabric. Using the same template, cut the smaller heart shape from glittery fabric.

Materials

* ½yd (0.45m) of red cotton fabric

* scrap of pink silk or cotton measuring at least 16 × 20in. (40 × 50cm)

* small scrap of lamé or lurex fabric

* sequins, faux jewels, and silver charms

* paper scrap or color photocopy

* 1⅜yd (1.2m) length of ⅜-in. (9mm) satin ribbon

* red sewing thread

* leftover lengths of embroidery thread

* 2yd (1.8m) bobble trimming

* fiberfill

* fusible interfacing (see Tips)

2 Pin and baste the glittery heart and the pink border onto one of the red heart pieces. Stitch ribbon and sequins to cover seams.

5 Clip curves. Turn the cover right side out, stuff with fiberfill, and slipstitch the opening.

3 To decorate the pillow, stitch jewels, charms, and the paper scrap in position by hand, using matching embroidery thread.

4 Pin and baste the bobble trim to the right side of the pillow front. Place back on top, right side down, and machine stitch all around, leaving a small gap in one of the long sides for turning.

Tips

If the fabric you have chosen has an open weave, you will either need to make a separate pillow form using the same template as the cover, or back the fabric with iron-on interfacing, to prevent the stuffing from poking through the weave.

Victorian

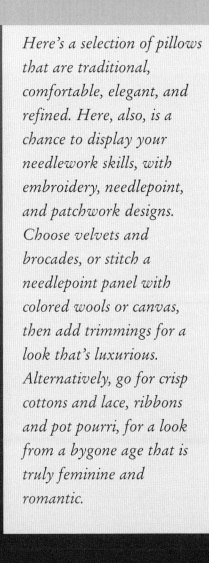

Here's a selection of pillows that are traditional, comfortable, elegant, and refined. Here, also, is a chance to display your needlework skills, with embroidery, needlepoint, and patchwork designs. Choose velvets and brocades, or stitch a needlepoint panel with colored wools or canvas, then add trimmings for a look that's luxurious. Alternatively, go for crisp cottons and lace, ribbons and pot pourri, for a look from a bygone age that is truly feminine and romantic.

Rose Potpourri

Make this enchanting little ribbon-bedecked pillow, and perfume your bedroom or boudoir with the subtle scent of roses.

As fragrant as it is pretty, this flouncy little pillow contains at its heart scented potpourri, just visible through a veil of net.

Satisfying to make, this project combines lace appliqué with a touch of ribbon embroidery and a tiny hint of the beadwork beloved by Victorian ladies.

The lace used here came from my grandmother's linen chest. A damaged table runner, destined to linger, unwanted, at the bottom of the pile, has been given a new lease on life. The undamaged bits of lace have been salvaged and reassembled to provide a lovely draped edging. The silk ribbon was also part of the original piece.

Rummage through old linen at a flea market to find similar materials.

1 Cut the main fabric into two equal squares to form the front and back of the pillow cover.

2 Center the square of net on the pillow front. Stitch firmly around three sides, fill with potpourri, then stitch the fourth side.

3 Stitch the straight edge of the lace to one edge of the ribbon. Cut this into four equal lengths. Place two of the pieces right sides together. Pin, then stitch at a 45° angle, to make a mitered corner. Repeat with the other pieces to form a square.

4 Pin the ribbon and lace "frame" on the pillow front. The ribbon will hide the raw edges of the net. Stitch in place along both edges of the ribbon but leave the lace free. Pin a line of narrow pink ribbon close to the edge of the net. Stitch in place. Cut the remaining pink ribbon into four equal lengths, tie each in a bow, and stitch in place at each corner.

5 Mark the positions for the embroidery on the satin ribbon using a vanishing marker. Draw the motifs by referring to the photograph.

6 Embroider the curved lines in satin stitch, using two strands of floss in the needle.

7 Stitch the foundation stitches for the ribbon roses using pink embroidery thread.

8 Thread the needle with embroidery ribbon and work the roses as shown in the diagram. Bring the needle up through the fabric near the center of the spider's-web foundation, then weave in and out of the threads until they are completely covered and a rose has been formed. Take the needle to the back of the work and fasten off.

9 For the leaves, thread the needle with green embroidery ribbon and work detached chain stitches (see Stitch Glossary, page 116).

10 Assemble the pillow cover. With right sides together, stitch front to back along three sides, with a 1/2-in. (1cm) seam

Materials

* 5½ × 5½in. (14 × 14cm) cotton net
* rose-scented potpourri
* 1⅜yd (1.2m) of 2½-in. (6cm) wide ivory lace
* ¾yd (0.7m) of 1-in. (2.5cm) wide ivory double-satin ribbon
* 10 × 20in. (26 × 52cm) remnant of ivory moiré taffeta fabric
* stranded floss, 1 skein each of pink and green
* crewel needle
* ivory cotton sewing thread
* embroidery ribbon, 1 card in each of the following colors and widths: forest green 2mm, colonial rose 4mm, rosewood 4mm
* 1⅛yd (1m) of narrow woven-edge satin ribbon in pink
* 24 clear pink glass seed beads
* 9½ × 9½-in. (24 × 24cm) pillow form

allowance, making sure you do not catch the lace in the seam and leaving a gap for turning. Clip corners, turn right side out, insert pillow form, and close opening.

Crazy Patchwork

Sumptuous silks and velvets, richly embroidered and embellished, conjure up the elegance of a Victorian drawing room.

The Victorians were fond of a type of patchwork known as "crazy" or "puzzle" patchwork. It became fashionable after the Great Exhibition of 1851 in London and was a marvelous vehicle for ladies to show off their skills with needle and thread – and a lovely opportunity to use up the skimpiest scraps of fine fabrics.

This pillow combines a wealth of fabric pieces, mainly silk with touches of velvet and lace, each edged with basic embroidery stitches and some embellished with embroidered motifs or bits of finery purchased from the notions counter. So dip into your scrap bag and see what you can find.

1 Beginning in one corner, baste a single patch to the muslin, using ordinary sewing thread.

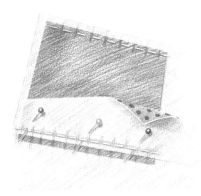

2 Arrange a second patch on top, right sides together, and stitch it in place.

3 Fold the second patch back, pin, and arrange a third patch on top. Stitch as before.

4 Continue in this way, covering raw edges of previous patches, until the background fabric is completely covered.

5 Cover the seams of all the patches with decorative stitching – herringbone, double herringbone, feather stitch, blanket stitch, etc. (See page 116 for basic embroidery stitches.)

6 On some patches, embroider a flower or butterfly, using the trace patterns on page 121. On other patches, stitch beads or buttons.

7 When the patchwork and embroidery are complete, make the pillow. With right sides together, stitch front to back along three sides, with a $1/2$-in. (13mm) seam allowance, leaving a gap for turning. Clip corners, turn right side out, insert pillow form, and close opening.

8 Add the fringe, positioning it over the seam line, and securing with small, neat stitches.

Materials

* 14 × 18in. (35 × 45cm) muslin
* approximately 50 small pieces of silk and velvet fabric
* small scraps of ribbon
* buttons and beads
* leftover lengths of embroidery thread
* 13 × 17in. (33 × 43cm) velvet fabric for backing
* sewing thread
* 12 × 16-in. (30 × 40cm) rectangular pillow form
* 1⅝yd (1.5m) tasseled fringe

Variations

For an authentic Victorian look, the colors used here are purples, pinks, blues, and black, with touches of red, green, and yellow ocher. Experiment with your own scraps by laying them all out before you start stitching, and choose the ones that harmonize best with each other. Even if your fabric pieces do not seem to go together, however, this patchwork technique has a clever way of unifying colors and textures, so be bold and brave with your fabric selection!

White on White

Crisp, lightly starched white cotton is the connoisseur's choice for a Victorian bedroom – complete with a family monogram.

What Victorian bedroom would be complete without a set of classic cotton bedlinen embroidered with monograms for that extra touch of class? Even if the rest of your linen is plain and unadorned, you could start by making a beribboned, decorative pillow with satin stitch initials and a simple flounced ruffle.

Choose crisp cotton sheeting, a length of cotton eyelet lace, and a narrow satin ribbon. The stitching is easy and relatively quick to do – and the effect is very classy!

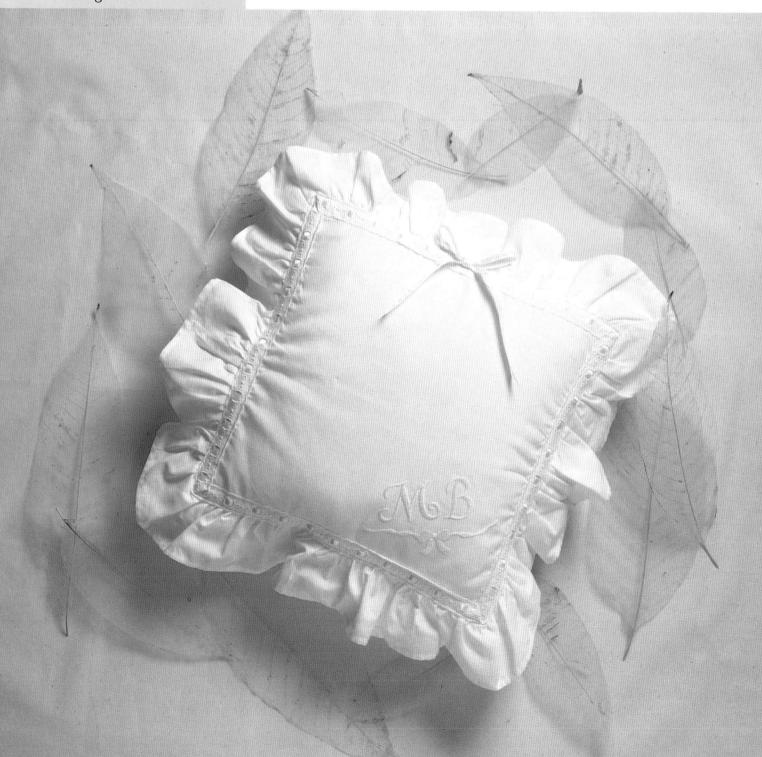

1 Cut a square of white fabric, measuring 15in. (38cm), for the front of the cushion cover. Cut two rectangles, each measuring 9 × 15in. (23 × 38cm) for the back. Cut a strip 60in. (152cm) long and 4in. (10cm) wide from the remaining fabric.

2 Trace your chosen initials from a book or magazine and transfer them to the pillow front piece, approximately 3–4in. (7.5–10cm) from the edge. Add ribbon motif traced from page 121, if you wish.

3 Stretch the fabric in an embroidery hoop and fill in the letters with satin stitch, using two strands of embroidery thread in your needle.

4 Join the ends of the long strip of fabric. Make a narrow hem on one long edge and run a gathering stitch along the other edge. Pull up to measure approximately 48in. (122cm), then pin in place

on the pillow front piece, easing gathers at corners. Baste, then cover the raw edge with eyelet lace threaded with ribbon, stitching firmly in place. Tie the ends of the ribbon into a bow, positioned at the top center of the pillow.

5 Hem one of the long edges on each back piece. Place back pieces on the front, right sides facing and with hemmed edges of back pieces overlapping slightly. Taking care not to catch the ruffle in the seam, stitch all around the pillow cover, ½in. (13mm) from edge.

6 Turn right side out through the center opening and insert the pillow form.

Materials

* *1yd (0.9m) of 90-in. (228cm) wide cotton sheeting fabric

* *1 skein of 6-stranded embroidery floss, in white

* *white cotton sewing thread

* *2yd (1.8m) of ¼-in. (6mm) satin ribbon, in white

* *2yd (1.8m) of ¾-in. (2cm) eyelet lace trimming

* *14-in. (36cm) square pillow form

Variations

When choosing lettering from a book or magazine, use a photocopier to enlarge small letters. Experiment by tracing the letters on to paper, then trace on to your fabric .

Tips

The opening at the center back of this cover can be left as it is, or you could add buttons or popper-snap tape to fasten. Whatever fastening you choose, bear in mind that bedlinen will need frequent laundering and so it should be easy to open and washable.

Fruit and Flowers Needlepoint

Truly elegant, this rich pillow with its dainty needlepoint picture seems to have been preserved from a bygone age.

Framed with damask and an opulent fringe, this pillow with its petit-point panel depicting roses, violets, grapes, and strawberries is the very essence of refinement.

If you are new to needlepoint or have no patience with long-term needlecraft projects, this pillow could have been designed just for you. The panel is relatively small and so takes little time to stitch, yet framed in this way, against a rich background fabric with velvet and extravagant fringing, it looks like a labor of love.

Materials

* *9 × 10-in. (23 × 25cm) 12-count canvas

* *tapestry yarn in the following amounts and colors: 2 skeins cream; 1 skein each claret, pink, palest pink, raspberry pink, dusty pink, gray-green, navy blue, dark green, green, pale green, bottle green, blue-green, yellow, strawberry, red, grape gray, deep purple, purple, violet, and white

* *½yd (45cm) of 48-in. (122cm)-wide damask fabric

* *30-in. (75cm) length of ⅜-in. (10mm)-wide velvet ribbon, in wine

* *matching sewing thread

* *13 × 14-in. (33 × 35cm) pillow form

* *1½yd (1.4m) fringed trimming

1 Using a single strand of tapestry yarn, work the design, following the chart on page 66. One colored square represents a single tent stitch or half cross stitch worked across one intersection of canvas threads. When complete, trim excess canvas to approximately ¼in. (6mm) all around.

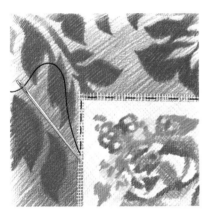

2 Cut two rectangles from the damask fabric, each measuring 14 × 15in. (35 × 38cm). Pin and baste your needlepoint panel to the center of one of these pieces.

3 Cut the velvet ribbon into four pieces, two measuring 8in. (20cm) and the others 7in. (18cm). Stitch them in place around the needlepoint panel to hide the canvas edges.

4 With right sides together, stitch front and back cover pieces together, leaving a gap for turning. Turn right side out, insert pad and close opening.

5 Add the fringed trimming, catching it to the pillow seam with small stitches and mitering the corners.

Tips
Use a small frame to keep the canvas taut while you stitch and it will be less likely to distort. See page 40 (Leopard Print) for more tips on working needlepoint.

DMC no.	Color
7745	cream
7431	yellow
7850	strawberry
7849	red
7590	navy blue
7245	deep purple
7242	purple
7243	violet
7396	gray-green
7345	dark green
7548	pale green
7540	bottle green
7861	blue green
7191	palest pink
7760	pink
7205	raspberry pink
7195	dusty pink
7207	claret

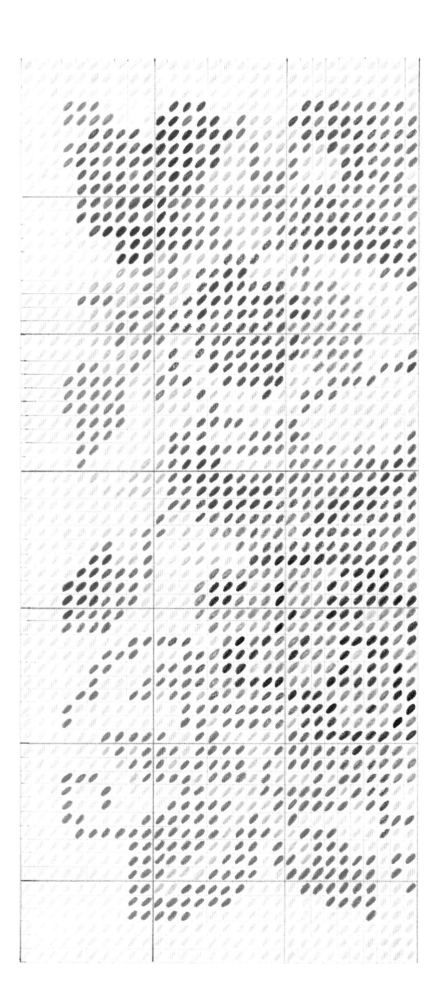

Woven Ribbons

Interlaced into a basketweave pattern, shining ribbons reflect the light in an enchanting fashion.

Ribbon weaving can produce satisfying results in next to no time. By experimenting with colors and widths, you can achieve different effects with just one straightforward method.

The Victorians loved to use ribbons to embellish home furnishings. Here, pale pink has been combined with a narrower violet satin ribbon and a rose-patterned jacquard, and extra trimmings in the form of ribbon rosebuds complete the picture within a rich velvet frame.

The only equipment you will need for ribbon weaving is a wood or cork board, and some thumbtacks or glass-headed dressmaking pins to hold the ribbons in place. The weaving is held in place with iron-on interfacing.

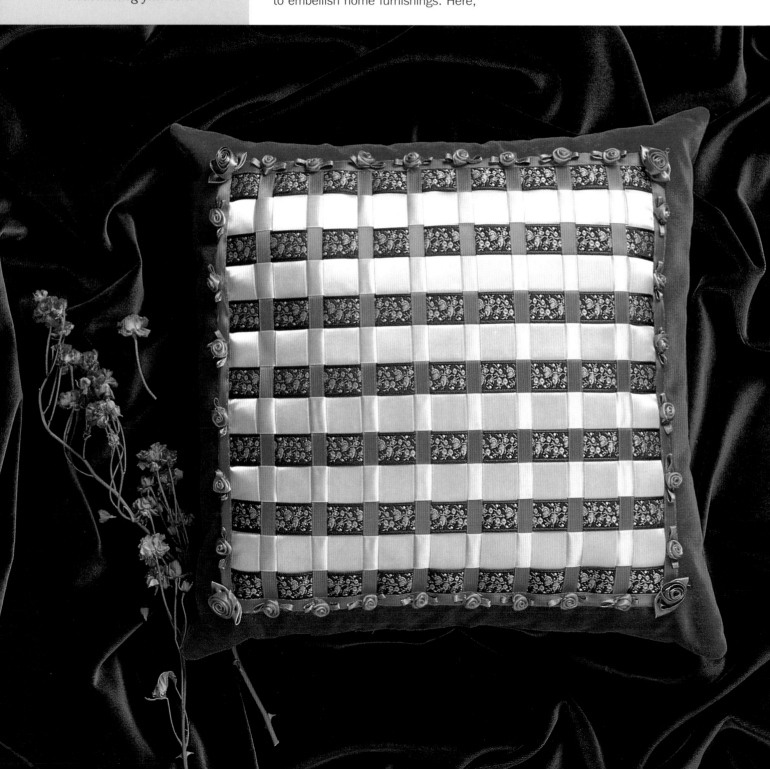

1 Cut the pink ribbon into 15 equal lengths. Cut the violet ribbon into 12 and the jacquard into 7 lengths.

2 Place the square of interfacing in the center of the board, adhesive side uppermost. Pin the vertical, or "weft" ribbons, to the top end of the interfacing, starting at the left side with a jacquard ribbon and then alternating pink and jacquard ribbons. The edges of the ribbons should touch each other without overlapping. Pin only the top end of each ribbon.

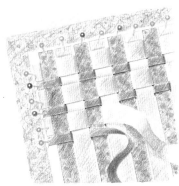

3 Starting with a pink ribbon, weave it under the jacquard ribbon, over the pink weft ribbon, under the jacquard, and so on until you reach the end. Push it gently to the top, then take a violet ribbon and weave it directly below, this time taking it over the jacquard and under the pink. Carry on in this fashion, as you weave each horizontal or "warp" ribbon, push it up next to the previous one and pin down each end to secure it to the board.

4 When the weaving is complete, press the work lightly with a dry iron on a medium setting to fuse the ribbons to the interfacing. Then take out the pins, turn the work over, and press the back using a hot steam setting. Leave to cool, then trim off excess interfacing and ribbon ends to form a neat square measuring approximately 11in. (28cm).

5 From the velvet, cut two squares, each measuring 15in. (38cm) for front and back of the cover. Place the ribbon weaving in the center of one of these squares, pin and baste in place.

6 To hide the edges of the weaving, pin, baste, and stitch remaining lengths of violet satin ribbon in place.

7 As further decoration, stitch on ribbon roses, referring to the photograph of the finished pillow as a guide to positioning.

Materials

* 13 × 13-in. (35 × 35cm) square of medium or lightweight iron-on interfacing

* 6yd (5.25m) of ¾-in. (18mm) wide single satin ribbon in pink

* 4¾yd (4.2m) of ⅜-in. (9mm) wide single satin ribbon, in violet

* 2¾yd (2.5m) of ¾-in. (18mm) wide jacquard ribbon

* ½yd (0.4m) of 36-in. (90cm) wide velvet

* matching sewing thread

* 28 small and 4 large ribbon roses

* 14 × 14-in. (36 × 36cm) pillow form

8 Assemble the cover. With right sides together, stitch front to back along three sides, with a ½-in. (13mm) seam allowance, leaving a gap for turning. Clip corners, turn right side out, insert pillow form, and close opening.

Tips

The finished size will depend on the width of the ribbons used and how tightly you have woven them, so allow for variations in measurements between your woven panel and the one here.

Lace Heart

Lavish with lace, this little pillow is a treasure – perfect to hold the rings at a wedding, or ideal for preserving a scrap from the bride's dress.

This little heart-shaped pillow is covered in a treasured scrap of Austrian lace from my wedding dress: fragile flowers and cobwebs preserved in a keepsake pillow.

To show the lace to its best advantage, choose a backing fabric that contrasts slightly. Here, white lace is backed with ivory moiré, but you could choose silk, satin, or velvet in cream, gray, pink, pale blue – or whatever you think looks best.

A pillow like this would make a glorious gift for a bride, to be used to carry the wedding rings to the altar and then kept as a memento. As a special touch, why not fill the pillow with a mixture of fiberfill and dried lavender flowers or potpourri?

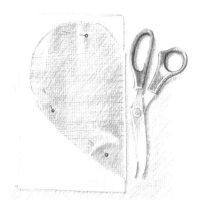

1 Cut the lace and the two pieces of backing fabric into heart shapes, using the template on page 120.

2 Place the lace heart on the front and stitch in place, using small, invisible stitches. Let the stitches follow the contours of the patterns in the lace, securing it to the backing fabric all over.

3 Run a gathering stitch all along the straight edge of the lace trimming. Pull up to fit the outside edge of the lace heart.

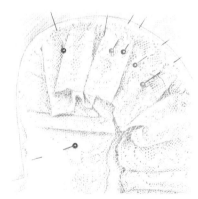

4 Pin and baste in place on the pillow.

5 Place the pillow back on top, right sides together. Pin, baste, and stitch the two halves together with a ¹/₄-in. (6mm) seam allowance, leaving one of the straight edges of the heart open for turning. Clip curves and turn right side out. Insert pillow form and stitch opening closed.

6 Cut the ribbon into three lengths: 19in. (48cm), 14in. (36cm) and 3in. (7.5cm). Fold the two ends of the longest piece to the center to form the loops of the bow. Lay this on top of the 14in. (36cm) length and stitch in place at the center. Fold under the long edges of the small piece and wrap it around the center to form the bow. Stitch ends, then stitch the bow in place at the center top of the pillow.

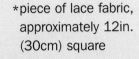

Materials

* piece of lace fabric, approximately 12in. (30cm) square

* 2 pieces of ivory or pale-colored fabric

* white sewing thread

* 1yd (90cm) of 2¹/₂-in. (68mm) double-faced satin ribbon, in white

* 1³/₄yd (1.6m) of 3-in. (7.5cm) wide lace

* heart-shaped pillow form (see Tips)

Tips

You can buy heart-shaped pillow forms ready-made, in which case you could use this to draw a pattern for your cover. Otherwise, trace the pattern on page 120 to make a pad from plain white fabric to fit this pillow. There is no need to alter the size. For more tips on making pillow forms, see page 14.

Alphabet Sampler

Here's a cross stitch sampler, not to hang on the wall but framed with fringe to display on a favorite chair.

Victorian girls produced samplers to practice stitching the letters used to mark fine linen. The alphabet here is quite a plain one, framed with a simple border and with some pictures added – hearts, potted plants, a figure, and a little house. It makes a

very fine pillow, the sort you will want to display in pride of place.

A rich fringe really sets off the embroidery. Choose one to match the evenweave fabric, or one of the colors in the embroidery – deep pink, old gold, or pale blue, perhaps. To back the pillow, choose a plain or patterned fabric of similar weight and composition to the evenweave. The stuffing is an integral part of this pillow; if you choose an appropriate backing fabric and fringe, the whole pillow can be hand-washed.

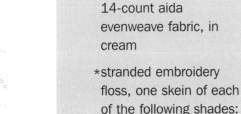

Materials

* *12 × 16in. (30 × 40cm) 14-count aida evenweave fabric, in cream

* *stranded embroidery floss, one skein of each of the following shades: green, lilac, pale blue, deep pink, old gold

* *tapestry needle no. 22

* *1⅝yd (1.5m) of fringed braid (see Tips)

* *sewing thread, in cream

* *42 × 20in. (105 × 50cm) medium-weight batting

* *12 × 18in. (30 × 45cm) backing fabric

1 Mark the center of the evenweave fabric. Stretch fabric in an embroidery hoop or frame and work the cross stitch design following the chart on page 122. One symbol on the chart represents one cross stitch worked over a single row of threads. Separate the strands of floss and use two strands in your needle throughout.

3 Cut the batting across its width into three equal-sized pieces. Place backing fabric wrong side uppermost, place the pieces of batting on top, and then put the embroidered fabric on top of the batting with the right side uppermost. Pin, baste, and stitch all the layers together around four sides, close to edges of evenweave fabric. Trim off excess batting and backing fabric.

4 Pin and stitch the fringe to cover raw edges.

2 Remove the completed work from the hoop or frame and press lightly on the reverse of your work, cushioning the fabric on a folded towel to prevent flattening the embroidery. Trim fabric to measure approximately 11 × 13in. (28 × 33cm) with a margin of approximately 20 threads of the evenweave all around.

Variations

Work your sampler on 14-count aida fabric, as here, to make stitching simple, or choose 28-count linen and work each stitch over two threads.

Tips

Choose a fringe like the one in the picture, which has a folded band that neatly encloses the raw edges.

Sweet Dreams

*Violets and dainty
forget-me-nots transform
a white pillow into a
romantic treasure.*

Just a whisper of embroidery can add oodles of character to a piece of bedlinen. This simple rectangular pillow is bursting with old-fashioned charm, provided by an embroidered corner motif that is easy to stitch.

The design, of a delicate butterfly with dainty stems of violets and forget-me-nots, is worked in pretty shades of blue, green, and violet complemented by a ribbon trim. To complete the picture, why not stitch the same motif on your sheets and pillowcases, too?

1 Cut two pieces of fabric from the sheeting, each measuring 12 × 17in. (30 × 43cm), for the pillow cover front and back.

2 Trace the embroidery motif from page 121 and transfer it to the corner of one of the fabric pieces, positioning it approximately 2½in. (6cm) from the edge.

3 Stretch the fabric in an embroidery hoop and stitch in satin and stem stitch, using the photograph of the finished pillow as a guide.

4 Mark a line 1½in. (4cm) from the edge, using pencil or an erasable pen. Using this line as a guide, position the raw edge of the eyelet lace.

5 Fold the corners of the eyelet lace edging into a neat 45° miter; pin and baste in position.

6 Stitch the mitered corners, trimming off excess and folding under raw edges to finish them.

7 Stitch the ribbon in place over the raw edge of the eyelet lace. Cut the remaining ribbon into four equal lengths, form each into a bow, and stitch to the corners of the ribbon frame.

8 Stitch the pillow front and back pieces together, right sides facing, pinning the lace back so it does not get trapped in the seam. Leave a gap for turning, turn cover right side out, insert form, and close opening with neat hand stitching.

Materials

* ½yd (45cm) white cotton sheeting

* 6-stranded embroidery thread, 1 skein of each of the following colors: violet, lavender, forget-me-not blue, pale green, apple green, honey yellow, creamy peach

* white cotton sewing thread

* 2yd (1.8m) of ⅜-in. (1cm) satin ribbon, in violet

* 2yd (1.8m) of 2½-in. (6cm) eyelet lace

* 11 × 16-in. (28 × 40cm) pillow form

Variations

The flowers, representing violets and forget-me-nots, have been stitched in naturalistic colors – but to match the color scheme of your room, you could work the design in different shades, such as peach and pink.

Tips

No instructions have been given here for fastenings. For a center back opening, follow the instructions on page 63 for the monogrammed pillow, adjusting the measurements accordingly.

Four Corners

Examples of embroidery, fabric painting and printing, weaving, and dyeing can be found in the four corners of the world. Whether your penchant is for bold, bright hues or the colors of nature, take your inspiration from another culture. Get out your knitting needles or dip your hands in a bowl of dye for some really creative, varied, and individual covers with interesting ethnic origins.

Guatemala Rainbow

All the colors of the rainbow combine in this warm and wonderful felted wool pillow with gay, gaudy pompom trims.

This colorful pillow takes as its inspiration the vivid, visually exciting woven textiles of Guatemala. The stripes, knitted in authentic colors, become slightly subdued when the fabric is felted – but bright touches are added in the form of wool pompoms.

If you like knitting, you will find it quick to produce the fabric for this pillow. Knitted in stockinette stripes, it couldn't be easier. If you are not a knitter, however, this is your opportunity to recycle an old wool sweater. To produce the felted effect, simply machine-wash the garment at a hot temperature, which causes the fibers to shrink and matt together.

1 With knitting needles and candy pink yarn, cast on 100 stitches. Working in stockinette stitch, one row knit, one row purl, knit striped bands as follows. Each band consists of seven two-row stripes, in two contrasting colors with a narrow black and white band (one row black, one row white, one row black) in between each colored band. Band 1: candy pink and yellow; band 2: raspberry and cyclamen pink; band 3: bright blue and turquoise blue; band 4: jade green and apple green; band 5: as band 2; band 6: purple and royal blue; band 7: as band 4; band 8: as band 1. Bind off yarn loosely.

2 To felt the fabric, wash in a washing machine at 140°F (60°C), with cotton towels to provide friction. Dry and steam press.

3 Cut diamond shapes, approximately 3in. (7.5cm) in diameter, from colored felt. Pin in place along center line of pillow front and zigzag stitch in place.

4 Add a small circle of yellow felt in the center and embroider petals using orange yarn and a tapestry needle.

5 Place pillow front and fabric backing right sides together, pin, baste, and stitch around three sides, approximately ¹⁄₂in. (1cm) from edges. Turn right side out, insert pillow form, and close opening.

6 With remaining yarn, make 12 large pompoms. Cut two circles of cardboard, each 4in. (10cm) in diameter, with holes 1¹⁄₂in. (3.8cm) in diameter cut out of the centers. Follow the instructions on page 80 for making pompoms. Stitch them securely to the pillow, three at each corner.

Materials

* wool yarn, one 1-oz (25g) ball in each of the following colors: candy pink, lemon, cyclamen pink, raspberry, bright blue, turquoise blue, royal blue, jade green, apple green, purple, fuchsia pink, orange, tangerine, emerald green, bright yellow, scarlet, black, white

* pair of knitting needles, size 8 (4mm)

* scraps of felt in bright pink, turquoise blue, yellow, apple green, and royal blue

* 13 × 15in. (33 × 38cm) backing fabric

* tapestry needle

* 12 × 14-in. (30 × 35cm) pillow form

Tips
To produce felted fabric, the yarn used must be good-quality 100% wool. Check the label. If it says the yarn is machine-washable, chances are that it will not shrink and matt, and therefore it is not suitable. Look for yarn that should be hand-washed at a low temperature.

How to make
Tassels & Pom Poms

Stylish accessories add a professional touch to both plain and exotic pillows.

Tassels can be simple or elaborate, plain or ornate – and very expensive to buy! They can add style and splendor to an ornamental cushion or just the right finishing touch to a homely one. Woollen pom poms are cheerful accessories for a knitted pillow. They are very easy to make, and add an authentic touch to traditional pillow designs, such as the Guatemala Rainbow on page 78.

How to make
Tassels & Pom Poms

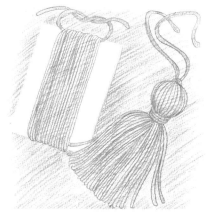

1 To make a simple tassel, cut out a piece of stiff card slightly longer than you want your finished tassel to be. Wind yarn round and round until you have a thick bundle. Tie it off at the top with a length of matching yarn. Cut through the yarn loops at the opposite end of the card then bind the tassel near the top.
To give your tassel a firmer, fatter head, insert a wooden bead or paper pulp ball before tying.

3 A quick way to make a tassel is to take a length of fringed trimming and simply roll it up. Secure by glueing or stitching.

1 To make a pom pom, cut out two cardboard circles the same size as you want your pom pom, then cut a small circle in the center of each of these. Place the two circles together, and wind the yarn evenly around this frame, until the center hole is completely closed up.

2 To make a multicolored tassel, unravel threads from a printed furnishing fabric. Alternatively, wind white thread, such as cotton knitting yarn, around a piece of card, then paint the yarn various colors, using fabric paints.

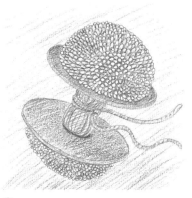

2 Cut around the outside edge, between the two layers of cardboard, and separate the two circles a little. Tie a length of double yarn round the middle of the pom pom and remove the cardboard.

Native Batik

Wild and wonderfully primitive in feel, this pillow features native African designs in earthy colors.

Based on traditional batik designs from Zimbabwe, this pillow is the perfect accessory for a room with such natural furnishings as rush matting, wood and cane. The pattern is made by drawing with wax on cotton fabric, then adding colored dyes. The "distressed" effect is then produced by cracking the wax, allowing dye to penetrate and create a marbled effect.

As with the silk painting on page 48, you will need to stretch your fabric on a frame. You might also like to invest in another piece of specialist equipment: a tjanting, which is a tool for applying hot wax. It consists of a brass bowl with a thin spout, attached to a wooden handle. The bowl acts as a reservoir, keeping the wax hot while it pours from the spout.

1 Mark a rectangle measuring 18 × 24in. (45 × 60cm) in the center of the fabric, using a water erasable pen. Within this, mark a 2-in. (5cm) border and fill this with diamond shapes, and a circle at each corner, using the photograph as a guide. Use the motifs from page 123 or draw them freehand.

2 Melt the wax in a metal container, keeping it hot over a low flame (see Tips).

3 Stretch the fabric on a frame, securing it with thumbtacks,

staples, or masking tape. When the wax is really hot, paint over the lines of the design you have drawn. Make sure the wax sinks into the fibers of the fabric and make sure that there are no breaks in the lines, to prevent color from leaking through.

4 Dilute the fabric paints with an equal amount of water, mixing thoroughly, and use them to paint the design. There is no need to let each color dry before beginning the next, as the wax will prevent colors from running into one another. Paint the diamonds in the border, parts of the flowers, and the lizard with sienna. Paint leaves and flower centers with chamois, then paint the whole of the background with fawn. Paint the circles and triangles in the border with black. Leave to dry thoroughly for several hours or overnight. Do not use heat, as this might melt the wax.

Materials

* *20 × 25in. (50 × 65cm) white cotton fabric

* *water-erasable pen

* *paraffin wax, approx 4oz (100g)

* *fabric paints, one 1½-oz (45ml) bottle of each of the following colors: 19 black, 25 sienna, 52 fawn, 53 chamois

* *1mm tjanting

* *paintbrushes

* *20 × 25in. (50 × 65cm) plain cotton backing fabric

* *matching sewing thread

* *18 × 24-in. (45 × 60cm) rectangular pillow form

Tips

The wax must be very hot in order to penetrate the fabric. If it is not hot enough, it will sit on the surface and the dyes will seep underneath the lines. Place a night light candle under a metal trivet, put the wax in a metal container such as an enamel cup or a clean tin can, and stand this on the trivet. When transferring the wax to the fabric, hold a pad of cloth under the spout of the tjanting to prevent wax from dripping onto the wrong places.

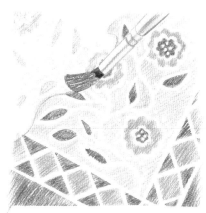

5 When the colors are dry, melt the wax again and, with an old paintbrush, paint the whole design area with wax, making sure it penetrates the fibers of the fabric. Leave to set for 10–15 minutes, then remove from the frame. Crumple the fabric in your hands, to crack the wax. Brush off any flakes of wax gently, then stretch the fabric on the frame again.

Tip
Any plain white cotton fabric is suitable for this technique. Here, bleached muslin was used. Be sure to wash the fabric thoroughly first, in order to remove any sizing that may prevent the wax from penetrating the fibers. Paraffin wax is available from craft and hobby suppliers.

6 Dilute the black fabric paint with a little more water and brush quickly and evenly all over the fabric. Leave to dry.

7 Remove the fabric from the frame and place on a flat surface. Scrape off any residual wax using a palette knife and taking care not to tear the fabric. Protect the surface with thick layers of newspaper, place the fabric on top, and cover with more newspaper. With a hot iron, press the fabric through the paper. The wax will melt and soak into the paper; at the same time, the heat will set the colors. Change the layers of papers frequently.

8 Machine-wash the fabric, then dry and press to remove creases.

9 With right sides facing, stitch front to back, following the outline of the design and leaving a gap to insert the pillow form. Trim seams and clip corners. Turn right side out. Insert pillow and close seam.

Right *You can use the batik methods described above and a range of different styles and subjects to create cushions to your own preference, either with a native style or a more contemporary look. These two cushions have been given floral motifs in bright, bold colors and patterns, to give a feeling of African sun and tropical vibrance to a plain wood floor and wicker chair.*

Sashiko Neck Pillow

Traditional Japanese quilting decorates a cube-shaped cotton pillow.

Dating back to the 17th century, sashiko is a method of quilting which originated in rural Japan, where it was used to make outer garments – coats, jackets, and aprons. The stitches bonded together two layers of cotton fabric, making a warm, hard-wearing cloth.

This little pillow combines the traditional dark blue cotton with white thread, and the six faces of the cube are an ideal way to display different classical quilting designs, both geometrical and free-form. This shape makes an attractive and practical pillow. Stuff the pillow form firmly enough to support your neck, but make it soft enough to be squashed into shape.

If you choose a fabric in which the weave is clearly visible, you can use it as a guide when stitching straight lines. Unlike the traditional Japanese method, only one layer of fabric has been used here, making this a very easy project. The stitch is running stitch – the simplest of all embroidery stitches – with the lines on the right side of the fabric slightly longer than the gaps in between.

Materials

* ¼yd (0.23m) of 48-in. (121cm) wide medium-weight cotton fabric, in dark blue

* 2 skeins pearl cotton in white

* sewing thread to match fabric

* 7½-in. (19cm) cube pillow form

* 8 ivory beads and 8 black seed beads

1 Cut the fabric into six 8-in. (20cm) squares. On each, stitch an outline square measuring 6½in. (16.5cm) in running stitch.

Use a vanishing or water-erasable marking pen to do this. Work running stitch along all the lines.

3 When all the squares have been stitched, join pieces with a ¼-in. (6mm) seam allowance. Leave one side open to insert pillow form. Turn right side out, place pillow form inside, and close seam by overstitching neatly.

4 To finish each corner, add an ivory bead held in place with a black seed bead.

Variations

Though blue and white are the traditional colors, this stylish stitching looks equally good on any colored background. Instead of a neck pillow, you could stitch a sashiko panel for the center of a square, round, or bolster pillow.

2 Within each outline square, mark a different pattern, based on squares, circles, or a freestyle design such as waves and fish.

Mexican Embroidery

Display your embroidery skills for all to see in this glorious, vivid floral panel.

The floral design on this pillow is based on authentic Mexican embroidery, the kind traditionally found on blouses. To recreate the look, it has been worked on crisp white cotton, framed with dainty pintucks and finished with a froth of cotton lace. Choose your fabric with care: pure cotton sheeting is perfect, bleached muslin thicker and more hardwearing, and voile more fragile.

Even an inexperienced embroiderer will be able to stitch this design, which is mostly satin stitch with lines of stem stitch. Stretch your fabric in a hoop and follow the instructions for the basic embroidery stitches. Just try to keep your stitching neat and even.

The button holes and old linen buttons have been made into a feature of this cover.

1 Transfer the embroidery motif from page 123 to the fabric. (For tips on transferring designs to fabric, see page 125.) Position it in the center of the fabric.

2 Stretch the fabric in an embroidery hoop. With two strands of floss in the needle, fill in the shapes with satin stitch, using the photograph as a guide to color.

3 When stitching the pansies, you can obtain a shaded effect by threading the needle with two different colored strands of floss and working long and short satin stitch.

4 When you have finished stitching, press the work, taking care not to flatten the embroidery. For the pintucks, measure approximately ⅝in. (15mm) from the edge of the embroidery, fold the fabric along this line, and press. Repeat on the other side. Make two more folds, each ⅝in. (15mm) from the previous ones. Press.

5 Stitch close to the fold. Open out and press pintucks away from the embroidery.

6 To assemble the pillow, turn under a 1-in. (2.5cm) single hem on the two long sides. Press. Fold top and bottom of the fabric to form a central panel (the pillow front) 11in. (28cm) wide. Press along these folds. Cut lace into two equal lengths and turn in raw edges at ends. Position lace between the folds. Baste in place.

7 Fold under 1in. (2.5cm) at each end of the fabric, and then another 1in. (2.5cm) to form a double hem. Stitch. Mark four buttonholes along one of these hems. Stitch. Stitch buttons on the other end to correspond to buttonholes.

8 Fasten buttons and stitch the two ends of the pillow cover, close to folds. Unfasten buttons and insert pillow form. Re-button.

Materials

* 19 × 27in. (48 × 69cm) white cotton fabric

* stranded floss, one skein in each of the following colors: violet, lavender, blue-green, green, lime green, yellow, bright pink, cyclamen pink, ruby red, orange, tangerine, turquoise blue, light turquoise

* crewel needle

* white cotton sewing thread

* 24in. (60cm) of 2-in. (5cm) gathered eyelet lace

* 4 buttons, ⅝in. (15mm) in diameter

* 12 × 14-in. (30 × 35cm) pillow form

Tips
Pressing the fabric at each stage will help to keep measurements accurate and give a neat, crisp finish.

Sunburst Tie-dye

Bright and beautiful, this soft velvet pillow is beaming with color and positively radiating happiness.

In many countries around the world – Africa, India, Pakistan, Thailand, Myanmar – the primitive technique of tie-dying is used to make simple patterns on cloth. Tie-dyed fabrics have been popular fashion items in the past generation, and if you have tried it yourself, it's a simple step from the tie-dyed T-shirt to this stunning pillow cover.

The vivid colors achieved with cold water dyes have been painted onto white cotton velvet, so not only does this pillow have maximum visual impact, but it's also soft and sensuous, too.

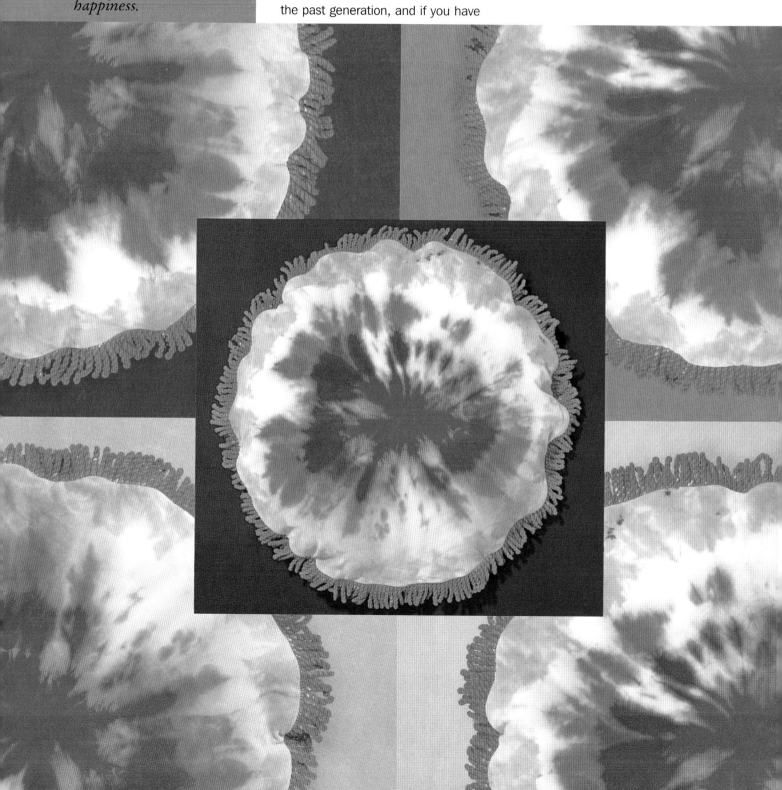

1 Wash the fabric and leave damp. Empty the yellow dye into a bowl or jug and add one sachet of fixative and 2¹/₂oz (60g) salt, or according to the manufacturer's instructions. Mix in a little hot water to make a paste, then add 1 pint (500ml) warm water.

2 Pinch the center of the fabric, then twist into a spiral. Secure with three rubber bands, dividing the fabric into four sections.

3 Paint the dye onto the outer section, pushing the dye into the folds of fabric with the bristles of the brush.

4 Mix the orange dye in a bowl the same way you mixed the yellow, and use it to paint the next section. Mix the coral color and paint the third section; then paint the central section with pink.

5 Place the fabric in a plastic bag, seal with a rubber band, and leave overnight.

6 The next day, remove the bag and the rubber bands, and rinse the fabric in cold water until the water runs clear, then wash and press.

7 Before disposing of the dyes, choose one to color the fringe – or mix two or more together to make the color of your choice. Pour this dye into a larger container, add enough cold water to cover the fringe, and leave submerged in the dye for an hour, then rinse and hand wash with hot water and detergent.

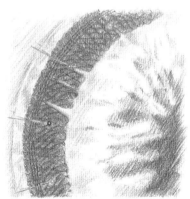

8 To make the pillow, cut a circle 24in. (60cm) in diameter from both the dyed and plain velvets. With the right side facing, pin and baste the fringe to one of the velvet circles, turning the fringe toward the center of the circle. Place the other circle of fabric on top with right sides together and stitch all around,

Materials

* ⅞yd (0.75m) of white cotton velvet
* ⅞yd (0.75m) of colored velvet, for backing
* cold water dyes: coral, pink, orange, yellow
* salt
* 4 sachets of dye fixative
* rubber bands
* paintbrush
* plastic bag
* sewing thread
* 22-in. (56cm) round pillow form
* 2⅛yd (2m) white cotton fringe

leaving a gap for turning. Clip seam allowance at intervals all around, turn right side out, insert pillow form, and close opening.

Variations

The colors used here have been chosen to reflect the sun rising or setting. The technique would, however, be equally effective with other color combinations. Try shades of blue and turquoise, or pink and purple, or other colors to reflect your own furnishings and decorations.

Provençal Prints

Printed cottons, cleverly combined, conjure up the mood and spirit of Provence in this comfy pillow with knotted corners.

The tied corners of this pretty, bright pillow are reminiscent of a carelessly knotted peasant scarf. The fabrics, in shades of red, green, pink, and blue, are Provençal in style and create an ambience of sunny southern France.

This is an easy cover to make. You simply join strips of fabric, add more at the corners – and *voila!* A stylish cover to brighten up your sun room, living room, or whichever room in the house needs a splash of Mediterranean color.

1 Cut nine strips of printed fabric, each approximately 2³/₄in. (7cm) wide and 19in. (46cm) long.

2 Join the strips with ¹/₄-in. (6mm) seams, press seams to one side, then trim to a square measuring 17³/₄in. (45cm).

3 Measure 1¹/₂in. (5cm) in from each corner, draw a line between the two points and cut off this triangular piece from each corner.

4 Cut four strips of printed fabric, each 2³/₄in. (7cm) wide and 8¹/₂in. (22cm) long. Join one strip to each corner. Press.

5 Cut a back measuring 17³/₄in. (45cm) from plain fabric, and join strips of plain fabric to each corner, as for the pillow front.

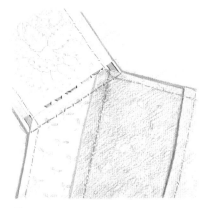

6 Join front to back, right sides facing, stitching a seam approximately ³/₈in. (1cm) from raw edges and taking seam line around strips at corners.

7 Leave a gap in one side for turning. Turn right side out, insert pillow form, and close opening. Knot the tab at each corner.

Materials

* remnants of printed cotton fabrics

* ⁵/₈yd (0.55m) plain cotton fabric, for backing

* matching sewing thread

* 18 × 18-in. (46 × 46cm) pillow form

Variations

You could make this cover in any medium or lightweight fabric, to match your own decor. Make the back and front the same color, or different colors, as here, to add interest to the knotted corners.

Folk Art Felt

Bright colors and simple shapes are a stunning combination found in folk-art designs around the world.

The flower and bird motifs on this pillow are based on a traditional Pennsylvania Dutch design, but the colors are the bright, primitive shades found in folk-art designs worldwide.

A dark background shows off these colors to perfection. In this case, a wool fabric in charcoal gray has been used, but you could choose black, navy blue, or dark green.

Since felt is easy to stitch as it does not fray and so does not need hemming, this project can be completed very quickly. You can buy felt in precut squares from most craft stores, and it is inexpensive.

1 Trace the motifs from page 124 and use them as templates to cut shapes from felt.

2 Cut the wool backing fabric in half and mark a circle 14in. (35cm) in diameter in the center using tailor's chalk.

3 Pin the felt shapes in position within the circle, then stitch in place using small, neat stitches.

4 Embroider details. Stitch main stems in chain stitch, and work details on leaves and petals in stem stitch and single, straight stitches. Use floss a shade darker than the felt.

5 Cut out pillow front 1¼in. (3cm) outside the chalked circle, making a circle of fabric 16½in. (41cm) in diameter.

6 For pillow back, cut fabric square in half. Fold back raw edge and stitch zipper or snap tape in place. Fasten. Cut into a circle, the same size as pillow front, with zipper in the center.

7 Pin and baste bobble trimming to the right side of the pillow back or front.

8 With right sides facing, stitch all around, ⅝in. (15mm) from edges. Clip corners, turn right side out through opening, insert pillow form and close fastener.

9 Topstitch ¼in. (6mm) from the edge, all around pillow.

Materials

* small felt squares in red, orange, yellow, blue, lime green, and bright pink

* ⅝yd (0.55m) of 36-in. (90cm) medium-weight wool fabric for backing

* matching sewing thread

* lengths of stranded floss in colors to match felt

* 12-in. (30cm) zipper or snap tape (see Tips)

* 1⅜yd (1.2m) of black bobble trimming

* 14-in. (35cm) diameter round pillow form

Tips

Fastening must be put in the center back of this cushion because, as the cover is topstitched, to form a decorative edging, fastenings cannot be inserted in the seam.

Felt is not washable, so it is not a practical choice for a pillow that will be subject to a lot of wear and tear.

Fair Isle Knitted

Practice your knitting skills on this winter warmer in soft, heathery shades reminiscent of a Scottish landscape.

In a corner of the British Isles, hand knitting has survived as a cottage industry for 500 years, with traditional patterns being handed down through the generations. The technique of stranded Fair Isle knitting, using two different colors in a row, produces characteristic patterns. Here, a few of the simplest of these patterns have been combined to make a delightful little pillow.

The design uses very little of each color of yarn and so is an ideal way of using up scraps from other projects. Choose a backing fabric of a similar weight and composition to the finished knitting, or knit back and front alike to make a double-sided pillow. Make tassels from leftover yarn, following the instructions on page 80.

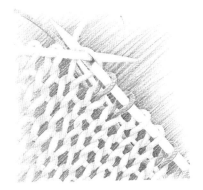

1 Using cream yarn, cast on 67 stitches. Follow the chart on page 125, working 72 rows in all, or until work measures 10¹/₂in. (27cm), keeping cream as the background color and using the photograph as a guide to the other colors. Bind off loosley in cream.

2 Using the tapestry needle, darn in loose ends. Press the work using a damp cloth.

3 Place knitting and backing fabric right sides together, pin, baste, and stitch approximately ³/₈in. (1cm) from edge of knitting, around three sides. Trim excess backing fabric and clip corners. Turn right side out, insert pillow form, and slipstitch gap closed.

4 Make four tassels from leftover yarn and paper balls or wooden beads and stitch one firmly to each corner.

Variations

This pattern would look equally effective worked on a dark-colored background instead of the cream used here. Try dark blue, brown, or black. To make a larger pillow, simply cast on more stitches and knit more rows! The number of stitches you cast on must be divisible by six, with one stitch over. This pillow is worked on 67 stitches – that's 11 multiplied by six, plus one. With a tension of 24 stitches to 4in. (10cm), the finished knitting measures about 10¹/₂in. (27cm). So, for a 14-in. (35cm) pillow, cast on 91 stitches; for an 18-in. (45cm) pillow, 109 stitches, and so on.

Materials

* lightweight 100% wool worsted yarn, 1oz (25g) of each of the following shades: cream, yellow ocher, blue-gray, stone, purple heather, blue-green, old rose, green, gray-green

* pair of knitting needles, size 8 (4mm)

* tapestry needle

* 12 × 12in. (30 × 30cm) backing fabric

* 10-in. (25cm) square pillow form

* 4 × ¹/₂-in. (13mm) paper balls or wooden beads, to make tassels

* tension: 24 stitches and 26 rows = 4in (10cm)

Tips

When knitting with two colors, hold both yarns in your right hand and strand the yarn not in use loosely along the back (or wrong side) of the work.
The method is basically stocking stitch – one row knit, one row purl – with stitches knitted in one of two colors along the row.

CONTEMPORARY

A new interior can be just the place to display traditional crafts to their best advantage. Patchwork, fabric printing, and appliqué take on a stylish twist with up-to-date colors and designs. Here is your chance to make a bold, bright statement in every room of the house, and an opportunity for the children to join in, too. Take up your needle and create a modern masterpiece!

Spots and Stripes

Transform a piece of white silk with sensational stripes and scintillating spots in a range of cool blue hues.

The technique of resist painting on silk is known as Serti. It involves painting a design with water-based gutta, then filling the shapes in between with silk paints. The colors soak through the fabric, spreading only as far as the gutta lines.

The only special equipment you will need is a frame on which to stretch the fabric before painting.

Gutta can be applied straight from the tube. Silk painting colors are mixable, but in this case, they have been used directly from the bottle, applied with a brush. Use any plain white silk. Silk satin crepe, as used here, is firm enough to be made into a luxurious pillow, backed with a printed silk fabric.

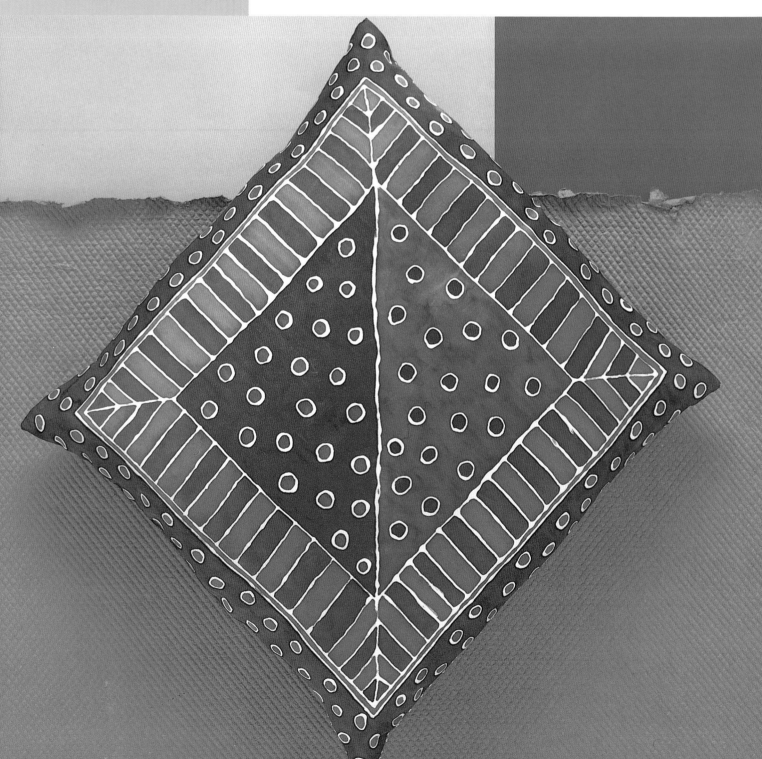

1 Mark a 20-in. (50cm) square in the center of the silk fabric, using a water-erasable pen. Inside it, mark a 15-in. (38cm) square, then another measuring 10in. (25cm) in the center. Divide the central square in half diagonally and fill each half with small circles, evenly distributed. Mark a border of stripes outside this, and add small circles to the outer border. Use the photograph of the finished pillow, opposite, as a guide throughout.

2 Stretch the fabric on a frame, securing it with masking tape.

3 Paint over the design you have drawn using gutta. Make sure the gutta sinks into the fibers of the fabric and that there are no breaks in the lines, to prevent color from leaking through.

4 Fill in the pattern with silk paints. There is no need to let each color dry before beginning the next, as the gutta lines will prevent colors from running into one another.

5 Leave to dry for several hours, then remove from the frame and set the colors by ironing on the reverse of the fabric for at least 3–4 minutes.

6 Leave for 2–3 days before washing to remove gutta residue, and leave to dry.

7 Press the fabric to remove creases and, with right sides together, stitch front to back, leaving a gap to insert pillow form. Stitch a zipper into the gap, or close with small, neat stitches.

Materials

* 24 × 24in. (60 × 60cm) white silk

* water-erasable pen

* 1 tube of colorless gutta

* silk paints, one 1½-oz (45ml) bottle of each of the following colors: 014 azure blue, 010 iris violet, 012 gitane blue, 011 navy blue, 013 cyan

* 24 × 24in. (60 × 60cm) silk backing fabric

* matching sewing thread

* 20-in. (50cm) square pillow form

* lightweight zipper (optional)

Tips

If you want a finer line, transfer the gutta to a plastic bottle with a fine tip. These, along with the gutta and paints, are available from most craft and hobby stores.

Bright Tulips

In colorful cottons, here is a big pillow to liven up the plainest chair or sofa.

By combining a few bright colors on a white background, these appliqué tulips make a bold statement, yet they remain fresh and pretty. This is a project you could easily tackle even if you are new to appliqué. The shapes are simple, and you hem the pieces before you apply them to the background fabric.

It is also a good opportunity to make your own colorful statement. Don't stick to the colors shown here, but see what your local store has to offer. You could have yellow blooms, crimson, violet or orange – or a clashing combination!

Materials

* *40 × 20in. (100 × 50cm) cotton fabric, in cream

* *large scraps of cotton fabric in red, pink, fushsia, green, and light green

* *2yd (1.8m) of 1-in. (25mm) bias binding

* *2yd (1.8m) of piping cord

* *sewing thread to match backing fabric and piping

* *18-in. (45cm) square pillow form

1 Cut the backing fabric in half, making two pieces each 20in. (50cm) square, for the front and back panels of the pillow. Cut the corners in a curve, using a cup as a guide for shaping.

2 Using the templates on page 124, transfer the stem, leaf, and flower motifs to the colored cotton fabric. You will need three flowers, three leaves (one in reverse), two curved stems (one in reverse), and one straight stem. Cut out the shapes around the outer line, which is the seam allowance.

3 On each shape, fold the seam allowance to the wrong side, clipping curves, and baste it in place.

4 Position the fabric motifs on the pillow front, and pin and baste in place. Using cream sewing thread, stitch each motif to the backing fabric, using small, neat stitches.

5 To assemble the pillow, cover the piping cord with bias binding (see Trimmings, page 16). Pin, baste and stitch in place on the wrong side of the pillow front, following the curve at each corner and with the stitching line ¾in. (2cm) from the edge of the fabric.

6 Place the two panels, back and front, right sides together and stitch again, following the first line of stitching and leaving a gap in one side for turning. Clip curves.

7 Turn the pillow cover right side out and press lightly. Insert the pillow form and close the gap with small, neat stitches.

Variations

Three different colored fabrics have been used for these tulip flowers, and there are two shades of green for the leaves. You may prefer to make all the flowers one color – red or pink, for example. A design of this simplicity lends itself very well to color variations.

Tips

Use opaque, medium-weight cotton fabrics for the appliqué. The seam allowance will show through thin fabrics and may spoil the result. In this case, back each piece with light-weight interfacing cut to shape using the inner line of the template. Stitch these in place on the backing fabric.

Finger Paints

Let tiny fingers loose with fabric paints and pens, then transform their pictures into plump little pillows.

Children are unselfconsciously creative. Instead of paints and paper, provide them with white cotton and "magic" dyes, and they can make their own colorfast pillows. Edith, aged three, drew a family portrait, while Lillie, six, produced a pair of mermaids.

Fabric paints, bought in small jars, are like poster paints and can be used straight, mixed together, or diluted. Fabric pens, like chunky felt tips, can be used to draw lines and details. For fine lines, use permanent markers, testing them on a spare scrap of fabric first for washability.

Use scraps of white cotton. Old sheets and shirts are perfect as their washed-and-worn surface provides a good base for the dyes. New fabric will have to be washed and pressed before you paint.

Materials

*scraps of plain white cotton fabric

*cardboard

*assortment of fabric paints and pens

*paintbrushes

*solid-color cotton fabric, for borders and backing

*matching sewing thread

*15-in. (38cm) square pillow form

*1¾yd (1.5m) piping (optional)

1 Cut a piece of cardboard to the size you want the finished pillow. Cut a piece of white fabric slightly larger than this – about 2in. (5cm) larger all around. Stretch the fabric over the cardboard, folding the edges to the back and fastening them with tape.

2 Paint your design on the fabric and allow to dry. Remove from the cardboard and press on the reverse with a hot iron, according to manufacturer's instructions.

3 Trim the edges of the painting, leaving a ½-in. (13mm) seam allowance all around. If necessary, add strips of colored fabric to make a border, thus enlarging the panel to the correct size – in this case, 15½in. (39cm).

4 Cut a pillow back piece measuring 15½in. (39cm) square from solid-color fabric. Place front and back pieces right sides together. Stitch all around with a ½-in. (13mm) seam, leaving a gap in one side for turning. Clip corners, turn right side out, and insert pillow form. Close the gap by slipstiching.

5 If desired, add piping around the edge, hiding the ends of the cord inside the seam at one corner.

Variations

Why let the kids have all the fun? Try copying favorite cartoon characters onto fabric to brighten up a child's room. If you are not confident of your skills as an artist, just photocopy the image you want to draw, enlarging it to the desired size. Tape the photocopy to a windowpane, tape the fabric on top, and trace, using a water-erasable or vanishing marker. Stretch the fabric, as described in step 1, and go over the lines with a marker pen, then fill in with color using fabric paints and a soft brush.

Squares and Bows

Bold squares and contrasting bows are pretty, unpretentious, and oh-so-practical.

When practicality is the keyword, why not make some simple slipcovers in bright fabric? These covers are straightforward to stitch and will instantly transform your pillows. Why not make a set and keep them on hand for a quick makeover?

Here, the pillow inside is glimpsed through the gaps in the ties, so two coordinating checks have been chosen. Pink and yellow are a fresh and pretty combination to bring a breath of sunshine into any interior. Choose washable fabrics for peak practicality and stitch ties from scraps or add ribbon bows for a softer, more feminine effect.

1 For the inner cover, cut two squares of small-check fabric, each measuring 19 × 19in. (48 × 48cm). With right sides together, stitch around three sides, clip corners, and turn right side out. Insert pillow form and close gap.

2 To make the ties, cut eight strips across the width of the remaining fabric, each measuring 2¹/₂in. (6cm) wide. Fold in edges and stitch. Tuck in raw edges to finish ends. Set aside.

3 From the large-check fabric, cut a strip measuring 37in. (94cm). Join short ends with a ¹/₄-in. (6mm) seam to make a tube.

4 Turn in 2³/₄in. (7cm) on each side to make a double hem. The width of the cover should be slightly less than the pillow – about 15¹/₂in. (40cm) – so that the cover underneath shows through at the sides. Pin in place.

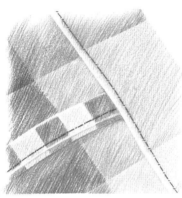

5 Before stitching, tuck the ties into the hem, four on each side, spacing them approximately 7in. (18cm) apart. Stitch hem, catching ties into stitching. Fold ties back over hem and stitch again, through all layers of fabric, to secure ties firmly.

6 Slip pillow into outer cover and tie the two pairs of ties together on each side.

Materials

- *24 × 55in. (60 × 140cm) medium-weight large-check fabric

- *20 × 55in. (50 × 140cm) medium-weight small-check fabric

- *matching sewing thread

- *18-in. (45cm) square pillow form

Variations

Instead of a contrasting check, use a solid fabric for either the inner or outer cover. This pillow would also look good made from two solid fabrics in bold colors.

Tips

When using woven checked fabrics, use the lines of the weave to guide you when stitching. Try to match the squares accurately at all seams for a professional finish.

Matisse Cutouts

These bright shapes and colors will look very familiar to followers of fine art, as this eye-catching design is an homage to the great Matisse.

When French Impressionist painter Henri Matisse began to make pictures from cut paper, could he have known that his work would provide such inspiration for others? Those gaudy cutouts, snipped with scissors from sheets of colored paper, have provided material for numerous graphic artists, illustrators, textile designers – and for this big, colorful pillow!

The shapes and colors have been taken from various pieces of the artist's work and assembled into one bright pillow cover. Where plain cottons of the right hue could not be found, white cotton was dyed with cold water dye to obtain the desired shade.

Though this is a large piece, it is relatively easy to make, and working with such vivid colors has an uplifting effect on the spirit!

1 Trace the motifs from page 123 and use them as templates to cut shapes from fabric. Refer to the photograph of the finished pillow as a guide to colors. On each shape, fold the seam allowance to the wrong side, clipping curves, and baste down.

2 Cut out four squares, each measuring approximately 12 × 12in. (30 × 30cm) from the bright blue, emerald green, red, and white fabrics.

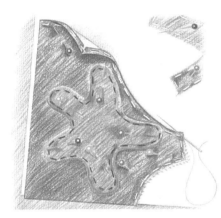

3 Start by stitching the marine blue corner shape to the white square, using small, neat stitches. On top of this, stitch the salmon pink flower shape, then stitch the marine blue star to the white shape, as shown. Cut a strip of shocking pink fabric, approximately 1¹⁄₂ × 10in. (4 × 25cm) and join it to the white square, by hand or machine, with a ¹⁄₂-in. (13mm) seam.

4 Stitch the lemon yellow shape to the green square. Join the green and white squares with a ¹⁄₂-in. (13mm) seam. Reserve.

5 Join the bright blue and red squares. Stitch the white star motif to the blue square and the bright yellow spiral and leaf shapes to the red square, overlapping the seam slightly, as shown.

6 Join the two halves of the pillow together and stitch the final blue and white pieces in place, positioning them over the seams.

7 Trim the piece to measure 21 × 21in. (53 × 53cm). Cut two strips of fabric, one marine blue and one shocking pink, each approximately 4in. (10cm) wide, and join to sides of square.

8 Stitch front to back, leaving a gap for turning. Clip corners, turn right side out, insert pillow form, and close opening.

Materials

* large scraps of colored cotton fabric in the following colors: bright red, shocking pink, deep salmon pink, bright blue, marine blue, emerald green, bright golden yellow, lemon yellow, white

* 24¹⁄₂ × 24¹⁄₂in. (62 × 62cm) plain cotton fabric for backing

* matching sewing threads

* 24 × 24-in. (60 × 60cm) pillow form

Tips

Use only pure cotton fabrics, which are easier to stitch than blends and form crisp folded edges. The measurements in the instructions are only a guide. Keep referring to the photograph of the finished pillow for positioning the motifs – and experiment with other colors and positions yourself to create your own unique work of art!

Envelope

This ingenious slipcover needs a minimum of sewing and will perform an instant transformation of any plain pillow.

Turn a simple remnant into a clever pillow cover with the aid of some bias binding. This snazzy slipcover is just a square yard of fabric edged with binding and tied over a plain throw pillow. If your sewing skills aren't up to much – or you are pushed for time – this could be the quick, easy answer to your soft furnishing problems!

1 Make the plain pillow: cut the chintz in half, making two squares each 18 × 18in. (50 × 50cm), for the front and back panels of the pillow. Stitch around three sides, 1in. (2.5cm) from raw edges. Trim seams, clip curves, and turn cover right side out. Insert pillow form and slipstitch opening closed.

2 Cut two lengths of bias binding, each measuring 1yd. Use these to bind two opposite edges of the striped fabric by hand or machine.

3 Cut the remaining bias binding into two equal lengths. Use these to bind the two other edges of the fabric, leaving 20in. (50cm) of binding at each end for ties. Folding these ends in half, stitch folded edges together by machine, or slipstitch by hand, using small, neat stitches.

4 To put the cover on the pillow, place the cover wrong side uppermost and place the pillow on top, lining up corners with center sides of cover. Fold corners of cover over pillow and tie opposite corners together at center.

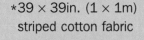

Materials

* 39 × 39in. (1 × 1m) striped cotton fabric
* 20 × 39in. (50 × 100cm) solid cotton chintz
* 6½yd (6m) of 1-in. (2.5cm) bias binding
* sewing thread to match chintz and bias binding
* 18-in. (45cm) square pillow form

Variations

There are some great creative possibilities here for combining solids with stripes. You could also make this envelope cover in checks, florals, or polka dots, to match your own decor.

Stars and Leaves

Print your own stylish fabric with a humble potato to make a cool, comfortable, floor pillow.

If you haven't made potato prints since you were a kid, then now is the time to try again – but this time use fabric paints, to create your own unique designer fabric. There are no special skills required. Anyone can achieve good results – and it's really fun to do.

1 Wash the fabric and leave wet. Mix cold water dye according to the manufacturer's instructions. Dye the fabric, then wash, dry, and press it.

2 Cut the fabric in half to make two squares, one for the front and one for the back.

3 Protect your work surface with thick layers of newspaper and lay out the fabric for the front. Tape edges to work surface so fabric lies flat and taut.

4 Mix blue and white fabric paints in more or less equal quantities – approximately two teaspoons of each – in a shallow dish and dilute with water to form a consistency like thin cream. Dip the sponge into the mixture and sponge the fabric all over to create a mottled effect.

5 Cut the potatoes in half lengthwise. Trace the leaf and star motifs from page 124 and transfer them to the cut side of the potatoes. Cut away excess potato, leaving the shape in relief.

6 Mix fabric paints to obtain the colors you want. Aim for a different shade of green for each leaf. Apply paint to the potato using the roller. Print one leaf shape at a time, in a random pattern, evenly spaced, all over the fabric. Leave to dry, then press with a hot iron on the reverse of the fabric, to set the dyes and make them colorfast.

7 Trim the two pieces of fabric, printed and solid, to 27 × 27in. (68 × 68cm). Stitch in a zipper or snap tape, if desired. Stitch around three sides with a ¹/₂-in. (13mm) seam. Clip corners and turn right side out. Insert pillow form and close.

Materials

* *1yd (1m) of 36-in. (90cm) wide bleached muslin

* *cold water dye, light blue

* *fabric paints: yellow, royal blue, white, green

* *sponge (see Tips)

* *roller

* *3 large potatoes

* *sewing thread

* *26 × 26-in. (66 × 66cm) pillow form

* *zipper or snap tape (optional)

Tips
A natural sponge is best for applying paint, as it creates a speckled effect. If you are using an artificial sponge, you may need to "distress" the surface by cutting little pieces out of it, using scissors, to create an uneven surface. Experiment by sponging paint onto a scrap of paper until you achieve the desired effect, before tackling your fabric.

Pointed Edge

Sharp points give clean, crisp lines to a bright Fifties-style pillow in smooth cotton chintz.

This small, square pillow with its oversized button trim has a retro style reminiscent of the 1950s, when bright scatter cushions were all the rage.

The pointed edging is quick and easy to do, fashioned from folded squares. The choice of fabric is plain chintz, bright in color and with a chic sheen. Here is your chance to mix and match the brightest of contradictory colors, to produce really striking effects for a modern interior.

1 From the red fabric, cut 24 squares, each measuring 4in. (10cm). From the yellow fabric, cut two squares, each measuring 14in. (35cm).

2 To make the pointed edging, fold each red square twice, on the diagonal, to form neat triangles. Press.

3 Join six triangles for each side of the pillow. With the folds all pointing the same way, overlap them as shown in the illustration. Pin and baste.

4 Attach the red edging to one yellow square. Match the raw edges and pin and baste in place.

5 Place the other yellow square on top, right sides together. Catch the edging in between, and switch all around, 1in. (2.5cm) from raw edges. Leave a gap for turning right side out.

6 Trim seam and clip corners. Turn right side out and insert pillow form. Close gap with small, neat stitches.

7 Cover each button with red fabric, following the manufacturer's instructions. Mark the central point of the pillow, then stitch buttons in place, one on the front and one on the back, taking the thread right through the pillow and pulling tight so the center becomes slightly dimpled.

Materials

- ½yd (0.45m) each of red and yellow cotton chintz
- two 2-in. (5cm) easy-cover buttons
- sewing thread
- 12-in. (30cm) square pillow form

Variations

Bright, contrasting colors like these are just right for a modern interior, but the pointed edging – sometimes called prairie points – can be used for pillows of other styles. Country-style might call for gingham checks or a pretty floral print, while romantics will doubtless desire shiny silks and satins.

Tips

Use a ruler and rotary cutter to cut accurate squares. Chintz makes clean, crisp folds: press them with a hot iron and a cloth before stitching in place.

Stitch Glossary

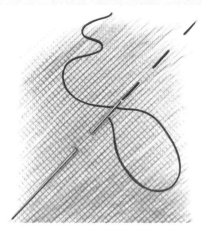

Running stitch The most basic of hand-sewing stitches, running stitch can be used for seams, gathering, quilting, and decoration. Keep stitches even. Use longer stitches for basting.

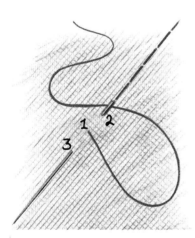

Backstitch Use this stitch for hand stitching seams or in embroidery where a fine line is required. Working from right to left, bring the needle to the front of the work at 1, insert it at 2, and bring it out again at 3.

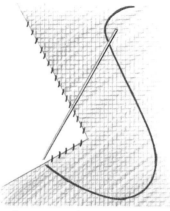

Slipstitch This stitch is used to close openings in seams and to attach pieces of fabric to a background in appliqué. Insert the needle into the background fabric and take a small stitch, then slide the needle inside the fold of fabric. Try to make the stitches as tiny and inconspicuous as possible.

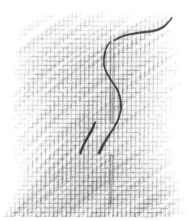

Straight stitch A single stitch, unconnected to any other stitches; can be used in embroidery or appliqué.

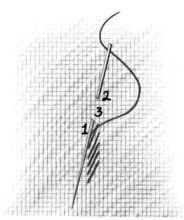

Stem stitch Bring the needle up through the fabric just above the stitching line at 1, take it back through the fabric at 2, and up again at 3. Continue working in this way along the line of your design, keeping the stitches small and equal in length.

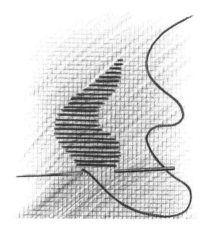

Satin stitch Stretch the fabric in a hoop or frame for best results. Stitches can be of varying lengths, but must lie flat to give a smooth finish with clean edges.

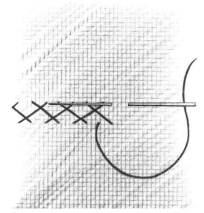

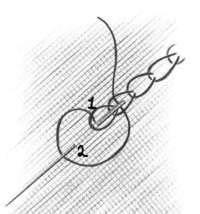

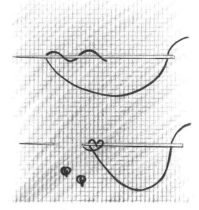

Herringbone stitch
This stitch is used for catching up hems and as a decorative embroidery stitch. Working from left to right, take small stitches from right to left, first at the top and then at the bottom.

Chain stitch
Working vertically, bring the needle out at 1, insert it back in the same place, and bring it out again at 2, taking the thread under the point of the needle before pulling it through.

French Knots
Bring the needle up through the fabric and hold the thread with your left hand. Twist the needle around the thread two or three times and insert the point back into the fabric. Pull to tighten the thread and form a knot.

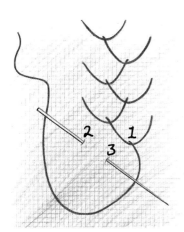

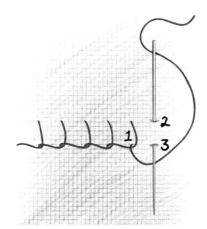

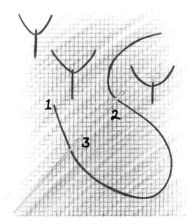

Feather stitch
This is an embroidery stitch which is often worked over a seamline in patchwork or appliqué. Working from top to bottom, bring the needle out at 1, insert at 2, and bring out again at 3, taking the thread under the point of the needle before pulling it through. Repeat in reverse at the other side.

Blanket stitch
Bring the needle up through the fabric at 1, down at 2, and up again at 3, having the thread under the needle. Pull the needle through to form a loop. The stitches should be evenly spaced and equal in length. This stitch can be used to secure the edges of appliqué shapes, for hemming, or as a decorative stitch in embroidery. Worked closely, it becomes buttonhole stitch.

Fly stitch
Bring the needle up through the fabric at 1, insert at 2, and bring it up again at 3. Do not pull the thread too tight or the fabric will pucker. Take the needle through to the back of the work again, forming a straight vertical stitch to hold the loop in place. Work as individual stitches, or in rows.

JAMES FORREST

Scottish Premier League
Saturday, May 1, 2010
Celtic Park

CELTIC 4

(McGeady 48, O'Dea 78, Forrest 87, Keane 90+2)

MOTHERWELL 0

James Forrest stole the headlines as Celtic stormed to a convincing 4-0 victory over Motherwell.

The 18-year-old winger slammed home a spectacular volley six minutes after coming on to the pitch for his first-team debut.

Forrest was introduced to the field of play on 81 minutes, replacing the opening goal hero, Aiden McGeady, and slammed home an impressive strike six minutes later.

CALLUM McGREGOR

UEFA Champions League second round qualifier
Tuesday, July 15, 2014
KR-Vollur, Reykjavik, Iceland

CELTIC 1

McGregor 84

KR REYKJAVIK 0

Manager Ronny Deila named a strong starting line-up in his first competitive match and handed a first-team debut to Under-20 star Callum McGregor in midfield.

McGregor's brilliant individual effort on 84 minutes was enough to secure victory in Ronny Deila's first competitive game. The youngster showed great endeavour down the right flank and cut inside his defender on to his left foot. He feigned to shoot three times before eventually unleashing an unstoppable effort, low into the KR goal to give Celtic the lead.

CAMERON CARTER-VICKERS

Scottish Premiership
Saturday, September 11, 2021
Celtic Park

CELTIC 3

(Carter-Vickers 64, Ajeti 70, 85)

ROSS COUNTY 0

New Bhoy, Cameron Carter-Vickers got his Hoops career off to a flying start by scoring the opener in this 3-0 win as the Celts maintained their magnificent home run in the SPFL taking their tally to 15 goals in three games.

The defender broke forward from the halfway line and unleashed an on-target shot from 25 yards that came off Jordan Tillson to loop over Laidlaw in goal.

It was a goal the scorer deserved for a composed and confident debut display in defence and his first real tackle of the game in the 13th minute raised cheers from around the Paradise bowl.

SEASON REVIEW
HOW THE LEAGUE WAS WON
JULY

TO say that July was a packed month for new manager, Ange Postecoglou is a bit of an understatement. There was little time to ease into his new seat as, on the games front, there were no fewer than eight to take in – five of those were friendlies, three at the training camp and two at home, as intentionally sparse crowds were tentatively allowed back into Celtic Park for the first time since lockdown.

On the competitive front there were ties home and way against Danish side FC Midtjylland in the UEFA Champions League qualifiers and a baptism of fire for the new boss with a first SPFL game away against Hearts at Tynecastle.

We already knew about Scott Brown, but he officially left that month and he was followed by Kristoffer Ajer and Marian Shved along with some youngsters and, while they were going through the out-door, coming in were Osaze Urhoghide, Liel Abada, Kyogo Furuhashi and Carl Starfelt.

MONTH'S MATCHES

F	N	Wed 7 July	Sheffield Wednesday	3-1 (Ajeti 31, Moffat 55, Edouard 89)
F	N	Sat 10 July	Charlton Athletic	2-1 (Dembele 24, Ajeti 39)
F	N	Wed 14 July	Bristol City	0-0
F	H	Sat 17 July	Preston North End	0-1
CL	H	Tue 20 July	Midtjylland	1-1 (Abada 38)
F	H	Sat 24 July	West Ham United	2-6 (McGregor 8, Christie 50)
CL	A	Wed 28 July	Midtjylland	1-2 (McGregor 48)
SPFL	A	Sat 31 July	Hearts	1-2 (Ralston 53)

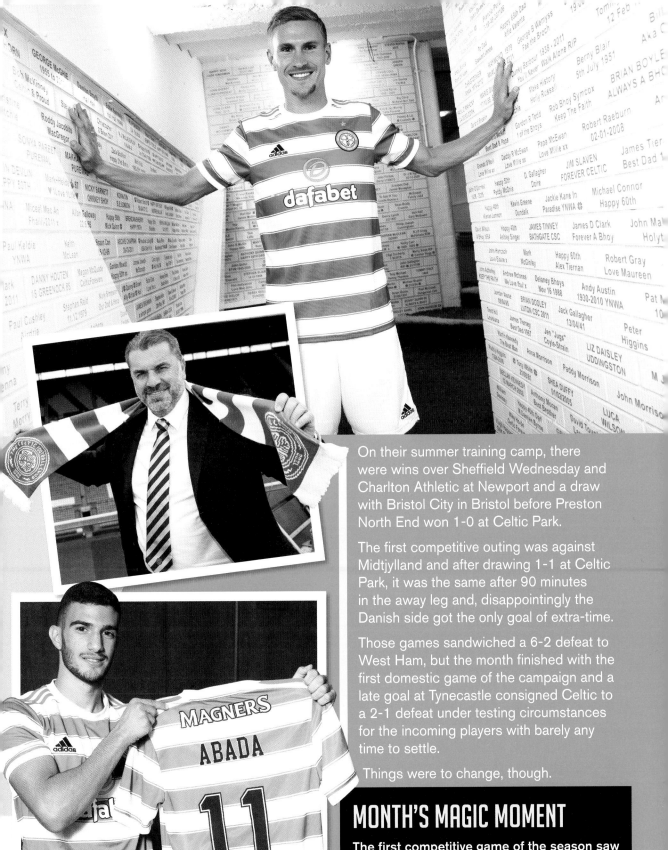

On their summer training camp, there were wins over Sheffield Wednesday and Charlton Athletic at Newport and a draw with Bristol City in Bristol before Preston North End won 1-0 at Celtic Park.

The first competitive outing was against Midtjylland and after drawing 1-1 at Celtic Park, it was the same after 90 minutes in the away leg and, disappointingly the Danish side got the only goal of extra-time.

Those games sandwiched a 6-2 defeat to West Ham, but the month finished with the first domestic game of the campaign and a late goal at Tynecastle consigned Celtic to a 2-1 defeat under testing circumstances for the incoming players with barely any time to settle.

Things were to change, though.

MONTH'S MAGIC MOMENT

The first competitive game of the season saw a Celtic Park bow for Liel Abada and the goal on his debut was also the first competitive goal of the new term.

The new Bhoy emerged as the goal hero in the 38th minute to score on his first outing. Ryan Christie forced a good save from the keeper with a left-footed shot and Abada was first to react as he darted in to smash in the loose ball.

SEASON REVIEW

HOW THE LEAGUE WAS WON

AUGUST

THE early-season transfer roundabout continued with Ryan Christie, Odsonne Edouard and Olivier Ntcham on their travels while Joe Hart, Josip Juranovic, Giorgos Giakoumakis and Liam Scales signed for the Hoops as did Jota and Cameron Carter-Vickers on loan deals.

And although the bulk of the new intake didn't arrive until the end of the month meaning their full impact wouldn't register for August, the Hoops who were available did exert their influence on the pitch with a string of impressive displays and scorelines.

First up were Czech outfit, Jablonec in the Europa League, and an away 4-2 win featuring Kyogo's first goal and a 3-0 home victory accounted for a 7-2 aggregate win to ensure progress to the next round where the Hoops would meet AZ Alkmaar.

Between those Jablonec matches, though, was the small matter of the Hoops' first league match at Celtic Park and the first

MONTH'S MATCHES

EL	A	Thu 5 Aug	Jablonec	4-2 (Abada 12, Kyogo 16, Forrest 64, Christie 90)
SPFL	H	Sun 8 Aug	Dundee	6-0 (Kyogo 20, 25, 67, Rogic 48, Ralston 83, Edouard 89 pen)
EL	H	Thu 12 Aug	Jablonec	3-0 (Turnbull 24, 53, Forrest 72)
LC	H	Sun 15 Aug	Hearts	3-2 (Edouard 29, Welsh 34, Kyogo 63)
EL	H	Wed 18 Aug	AZ Alkmaar	2-0 (Kyogo 12, Forrest 61)
SPFL	H	Sat 21 Aug	St Mirren	6-0 (Abada 17, 22, Turnbull 28, 44, 84, Edouard 62)
EL	A	Thu 26 Aug	AZ Alkmaar	1-2 (Kyogo 3)
SPFL	A	Sun 29 Aug	Rangers	0-1

SPFL meeting with fans at the ground since the start of lockdown. The Celts didn't hold back as Dundee were hit for six with Kyogo bringing the house down with a hat-trick.

It was 'as you were' for the next league action at home with another 6-0 win, this time over St Mirren and this time with David Turnbull on hat-trick duty. There was a fortnight between those 6-0 wins, though, and aside from tying up the Jablonec outcome, the Hoops also gained a measure of payback against Hearts with a fine 3-1 League Cup win as well as a 2-0 win over AZ Alkmaar in the Europa League.

A 2-1 defeat over in The Netherlands in the second leg was followed a few days later with a tight 1-0 defeat at Ibrox, but UEFA Europa League group-stage football had been confirmed with the 3-2 aggregate win and the signs were there that the manager's style of play was registering with the team and they were starting to deliver.

MONTH'S MAGIC MOMENT

Ange Postecoglou's Celtic side marked their first home league game of the campaign with an outstanding display of attacking football that saw them hit six goals without reply against Dundee.

On an afternoon of many impressive performances, it was hat-trick hero, Kyogo, who picked up the Man of the Match award for his stunning goalscoring feat.

And no one would argue that the Japanese attacker deserved the accolade, though every one of his team-mates were also in top form to take all three points.

SEASON REVIEW
HOW THE LEAGUE WAS WON
SEPTEMBER

THE month of September threw up six games in three competitions and the month, as well as his Celtic career, got off to a flier for defender, Cameron Carter-Vickers who had arrived on loan from Spurs just as the transfer deadline neared.

Ross County were the visitors and the Highland outfit were holding the Celts to 0-0 until the 64th minute when a speculative shot from the new Celt put the Hoops in front with the aid of a deflection. Albian Ajeti added two more goals to give the Celts a comfortable 3-0 win in the first game of the month.

There was a sensational start to Celtic's UEFA Europa League Group G encounters when they travelled to Seville and took a quick 2-0 lead over La Liga side, Real Betis. However, by early in the second half, the home side were 4-2 in front and an 87th-minute goal from Anthony Ralston gave the Hoops hope, but it finished 4-3 despite an inspiring display from the Celts that deserved more.

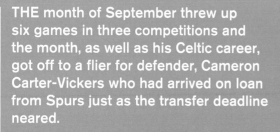

MONTH'S MATCHES

SPFL	H	Sat 11 Sep	ROSS COUNTY	3-0 (Carter-Vickers 64, Ajeti 70, 85)
EL	A	Thu 16 Sep	REAL BETIS	3-4 (Ajeti 13, Juranovic 27 pen, Ralston 87)
SPFL	A	Sun 19 Sep	LIVINGSTON	0-1
LC	H	Thu 23 Sep	RAITH ROVERS	3-0 (Jota 26, Abada 40, Turnbull 47)
SPFL	H	Sun 26 Sep	DUNDEE UTD	1-1 (Abada 16)
EL	H	Thu 30 Sep	BAYER 04	0-4

In Celtic's home European tie in the last game of the month, Bundesliga outfit, Bayer Leverkusen led 2-0 at the break, with a penalty and a last goal deep into injury time handing the German side a 4-0 win on a night when, once again on the European stage, the Celts deserved more from the game for their performance.

In the league, Livingston parked the bus on their artificial surface and held out for a win thanks to their 25th-minute goal and, a week later, Dundee United visited Celtic Park and left with a 1-1 draw despite the Hoops hitting the woodwork three times and creating numerous other gilt-edged chances.

Between those two games, though, Raith Rovers arrived on League Cup duty and Jota got his first goal in the Hoops as a 3-0 win over the Fife side took the Hoops through to a semi-final tie against St Johnstone at Hampden.

MONTH'S MAGIC MOMENT

United States internationalist, Cameron Carter-Vickers got his Celtic career off to the best possible start on his arrival from Tottenham Hotspur by netting on his debut in the opening game of the month when Ross County arrived on league duty.

The 3-0 scoreline may not have been as spectacular as the two opening home SPFL 6-0 encounters against Dundee and St Mirren, but the 3-0 win was celebrated just as much, and none more so than by Carter-Vickers.

He netted the opener in the 64th minute when his goal-bound shot ricocheted off Jordan Tillson and still made its way into the back of the net for the defender's dream debut.

SEASON REVIEW
HOW THE LEAGUE WAS WON
OCTOBER

ONCE more, there were six games in October but this time there was no holding the Celts back as a 0-0 draw with Livingston in the final game of the month was the only blip on an otherwise green-glowing radar.

It started off with a potentially difficult trip to Pittodrie where Scott Brown and Aberdeen awaited, but Kyogo's eighth goal of the term and Jota's crucial winner in the 2-1 outcome paved the way for history to repeat itself when Ange Postecoglou took the acclaim of the travelling support in the Granite City.

Following the international break, two stunning goals gave the Hoops a 2-0 win over Motherwell at Fir Park, and a few days later they recorded the same scoreline on the European front when Ferencvaros were the visitors on Group G duty.

It was then three-in-a-row as far as 2-0 scorelines go when St Johnstone visited and Giorgos Giakoumakis marked his

MONTH'S MATCHES

SPFL	A	Sun 3 Oct	Aberdeen	2-1 (Kyogo 11, Jota 84)
SPFL	A	Sat 16 Oct	Motherwell	2-0 (Jota 17, Turnbull 52)
EL	H	Tue 19 Oct	Ferencvaros	2-0 (Kyogo 57, Turnbull 81)
SPFL	H	Sat 23 Oct	St Johnstone	2-0 (Giakoumakis 34, Juranovic 80 pen)
SPFL	A	Wed 27 Oct	Hibernian	3-1 (Ralston 9, Carter-Vickers 13, Kyogo 30)
SPFL	H	Sat 30 Oct	Livingston	0-0

first Celtic start with his first goal and Josip Juranovic added another to close the scoring for the day.

Next up was another potentially hazardous trip to a venue where the Celts hadn't won in nearly eight years – Easter Road. However, a whirlwind start by the Hoops had them 3-0 up after only half-an-hour's play and although Hibernian pulled one back, there was no denying that the classy Celts were always in command.

MONTH'S MAGIC MOMENT

The five wins were bookended by significant wins at Pittodrie and Easter Road, so the Magic Moments were beginning to mount up, but the Motherwell game at Fir Park produced two simply superb goals.

The first came after Kyogo won the ball halfway back in the Celtic half and ended when Tom Rogic picked out the on-running Jota who fired in an unstoppable left-foot shot on the angle from 12 yards.

The second was a peach as David Turnbull let loose with a right-foot shot from 30 yards that screamed into the net for the 2-0 win.

SEASON REVIEW
HOW THE LEAGUE WAS WON
NOVEMBER

THE month of November got off to the best possible start when a 3-2 victory over Ferencvaros in Budapest guaranteed European football after the New Year and kept the Hoops in the hunt for a Europa League place.

The goals came from Kyogo, Jota and Liel Abada as the Celts did what they had to do on the night and looked to keep the fight going in their next Group G outing – the toughest one of the lot in facing Bayer Leverkusen on their own patch.

Twice Celtic took the lead in the game against the Bundesliga outfit on German soil and twice the home side came back before delivering the cruellest of blows – an 87th-minute winner for Leverkusen consigned the Celts to the Europa Conference League rather than its big brother, but, once more, Ange Postecoglou's side could be proud of their European display.

Between those two European ties were two fine wins in two domestic competitions as Dundee and St Johnstone were defeated in the league and League Cup respectively.

MONTH'S MATCHES

EL	A	Thu 4 Nov	Ferencvaros	3-2 (Kyogo 2, Jota 23, Abada 59)
SPFL	A	Sun 7 Nov	Dundee	4-2 (Jota 8, 47, Kyogo 19, 50)
LC	N	Sat 20 Nov	St Johnstone	1-0 (Forrest 73)
EL	A	Thu 25 Nov	Bayer 04	2-3 (Juranovic pen 40, Jota 56)
SPFL	H	Sun 28 Nov	Aberdeen	2-1 (Jota 19, McGregor 60)

The first of those games saw a trip to Dens Park where Jota and Kyogo shared the goals equally in a 4-2 win over Dundee to bring home another three SPFL points. Meanwhile, the National Stadium was the destination for Celtic in their League Cup semi-final meeting with holders

MONTH'S MAGIC MOMENT

Following four years of the Celts winning the Treble, with both domestic cups as part of the tally, it was St Johnstone who took up the mantle by being the surprise winners of the League Cup and Scottish Cup double in Season 2020/21.

And it was Celtic who came up against the then League Cup holders at the semi-final stage last season in Ange Postecoglou's first game at Hampden.

It was a tight game, but a goal from James Forrest paved the way for a return to the National Stadium in December when more Celtic and Ange Postecoglou history would be written.

St Johnstone, and it was James Forrest on target in the 1-0 win that put the Hoops through to meet Hibernian in the final.

Following the Leverkusen game came the final match of the month and the occasion was shrouded in sadness as Celtic Park celebrated the life of Lisbon Lion, Bertie Auld as this was the first home game since his sad passing.

Both captains, Callum McGregor and Scott Brown, laid wreaths before the match as the crowd took part in a touching tribute to one of the most loved and revered Celts.

And the Hoops on the pitch also paid tribute to Bertie with an entertaining 2-1 win with McGregor netting the winner after Aberdeen had equalised from the spot.

SEASON REVIEW
HOW THE LEAGUE WAS WON
DECEMBER

IN a packed schedule for the month, each and every game had its own importance, but one stood out from the bunch – the one that would deliver the best Christmas present of them all, and the one that presented Ange Postecoglou with the opportunity to win silverware at the very first time of asking.

It was the League Cup final at Hampden on December 19 with Hibernian looking to stop the Hoops from lifting the trophy for the 20th time.

They looked like they might just do it as well when they took the lead in the 50th minute – but they had barely stopped celebrating when Kyogo fired in the equaliser, then, 20 minutes later, he lobbed in the killer blow.

Ange's Celts had won 2-1 and the first silverware of the season was in the bag – the Aussie had lifted a trophy at the very first time of asking.

MONTH'S MATCHES

SPFL	H	Thu 2 Dec	Hearts	1-0 (Kyogo 33)
SPFL	A	Sun 5 Dec	Dundee Utd	3-0 (Rogic 19, Turnbull 40, Scales 81)
EL	H	Thu 9 Dec	Real Betis	3-2 (Welsh 3, Henderson 72, Turnbull 78 pen)
SPFL	H	Sun 12 Dec	Motherwell	1-0 (Rogic 45)
SPFL	A	Wed 15 Dec	Ross County	2-1 (Abada 21, Ralston 90+7)
LC	N	Sun 19 Dec	Hibernian	2-1 (Kyogo 52, 72)
SPFL	A	Wed 22 Dec	St Mirren	0-0
SPFL	A	Sun 26 Dec	St Johnstone	3-1 (Abada 9, 22, Bitton 82)

WINNERS 2021/22

individual effort from Tom Rogic delivered all three points in a 1-0 home win over Motherwell before, in the next game, one of the most tense finales to a Celtic match in years.

Victoria Park was the midweek venue and, with Ross County equalising and the Celts down to 10 men, the clock was ticking away and nothing seemed to be going right. At least that was the case until seven minutes into injury time when Anthony Ralston headed home the most dramatic of winners.

Following the League Cup final, the Celts were scheduled to face up to both Saints in the shape of St Mirren and St Johnstone with the Paisley match ending 0-0 before Celtic's Israeli duo came to the fore by netting the goals in a 3-1 win at Perth.

December, as usual, was a packed month with nine games squeezed in, and away from the League Cup final, there were four SPFL wins surrounding our last UEFA Europa League match at home against Real Betis.

This game was charged with being a 'dead rubber' but try telling that to the young Celtic starting line-up that went out and defeated the La Liga outfit 3-2 to celebrate going into the Europa Conference League with a win against top opposition.

And the league games weren't without excitement as a 1-0 home win over Hearts was followed by a resounding and stylish 3-0 win over Dundee United at Tannadice, then following the Euro game, a fantastic

MONTH'S MAGIC MOMENT

There were many magic moments with eight games in an unbeaten month in all competitions, so there are many candidates to choose from.

The League Cup win was an obvious contender, but the impact and relief of Anthony Ralston's 90th-minute winner in Dingwall registered on the Richter scale, so that will live long in the memory of many.

However, the importance of finishing the calendar year with a win to set up the Celts for their return to action in mid-January, thanks to the 3-1 away victory over St Johnstone, cannot be underestimated.

SEASON REVIEW

HOW THE LEAGUE WAS WON

JANUARY

THE Scottish Cup and a 2-1 win over Alloa Athletic gave some respite and a bit of a breather from three crucial league games that were all equally breath-taking, and each for different reasons, as the Hoops hiked up the pressure in the league.

Before a ball was kicked, though, the new Japanese trio of Reo Hatate, Daizen Maeda and Yosuke Ideguchi had arrived among much excitement, and they would soon be followed by Matt O'Riley from MK Dons.

The first match back had a European feel about it as a jam-packed Paradise under the Monday-night lights welcomed the new Bhoys for the first time, and the rest of the Celts for the first game after the winter break – and it was one of the new intake who brought the house down after only five minutes as Maeda made an immediate impact as a Celt with the first goal in a 2-1 win.

The following night, Rangers drew 1-1 with Aberdeen and the gap was down to five points.

The next midweek was just as memorable, as a rocket-shot from Hatate opened the scoring in a 2-1 win over Hearts at

MONTH'S MATCHES

SPFL	H	Mon 17 Jan	Hibernian	2-0 (Maeda 5, Juranovic 25 pen)
SC	A	Sat 22 Jan	Alloa Athletic	2-1 (Giakoumakis 14, Abada 45)
SPFL	A	Wed 26 Jan	Hearts	2-1 (Hatate 27, Giakoumakis 35)
SPFL	H	Sat 29 Jan	Dundee Utd	1-0 (Abada 90)

Tynecastle, which was made even more nail-biting as, 10 minutes after he brought it back to 2-1, a penalty from Liam Boyce cracked off the inside of the left-hand post, curled along the face of the goal inches from the line and went out at the other end for a by-kick.

A few days later, Celtic sort of repeated the late show from the previous month when a 10-man Hoops side netted the winner in the last minute, this time against Dundee United at Paradise.

Just when all looked lost, Jota was played in down the right and he chipped it into the area for Liel Abada, who with all the pressure on him was the coolest customer in the stadium, controlling the cross and smashing it into the top left corner from close range.

The tension release was palpable, as, earlier that day, another 90th-minute goal set the wheels in motion for the coming week. That goal gave Ross County a 3-3 draw with Rangers, and the month that started with Celtic being six points off the pace saw the gap narrowed to just two points, just in time for the first game of February – a midweek derby meeting at Paradise.

MONTH'S MAGIC MOMENT

Yet again, this was a month stuffed to the gunwales with magical moments from the signing of the new intake to picking up the nine points available in three fully absorbing SPFL games with each of them having their own electric moments.

Daizen Maeda's opener against Hibs, Reo Hatate's stunner against Hearts – they were both scored amid bubbling atmospheres as Ange Postecoglou's side continued to batt off all challenges.

However, due to its importance in the bigger picture of what was to unfold over the following week, it has to be Liel Abada's late show at Celtic Park as the 10-man Hoops earned all three points with a 90th-minute winner.

For all the world it seemed like one of those afternoons, with Nir Bitton sent off late on and the Celts missing chance after chance. But in typical Celtic fashion, with hearts racing and the nerves wrangling, up stepped Abada right on the stroke of full time to win it and send Paradise into overdrive.

SEASON REVIEW

HOW THE LEAGUE WAS WON

FEBRUARY

THERE were eight matches in three competitions this month, but it was all about the very first game – or the very first 44 minutes to be more precise.

Just like the first game of the previous month, this was a midweek match under the lights and this was a derby head-to-head of the tallest order – the winners at the end of the night would be top of the league.

The six-point gap had been cut to just two, and the cauldron of Paradise awaited the contenders, but, with barely five minutes on the clock, a clear indication of how this game was going to end up was given when Reo Hatate fired the Hoops into an early lead.

The Japanese star all but killed the game three minutes before the break when he fired in a belter of a goal, again from outside the box, and, just two minutes after that, he sent over a teasing cross that Liel Abada was on in a flash, and from between two defenders he skelped in number three.

MONTH'S MATCHES

SPFL	H	Wed 2 Feb	Rangers	3-0 (Hatate 5, 42, Abada 44)
SPFL	A	Sun 6 Feb	Motherwell	4-0 (Abada 28, Rogic 31, 45, Maeda 71)
SPFL	A	Wed 9 Feb	Aberdeen	3-2 (Jota 16, 62, O'Riley 20)
SC	H	Sun 13 Feb	Raith Rovers	4-0 (Scales 22, Giakoumakis 68, Maeda 71, Bitton 88)
EC	H	Thu 17 Feb	Bodø/Glimt	1-3 (Maeda 79)
SPFL	H	Sun 20 Feb	Dundee	3-2 (Giakoumakis 34, 38, 86)
EC	A	Thu 24 Feb	Bodø/Glimt	0-2
SPFL	A	Sun 27 Feb	Hibernian	0-0

That, allied with an earlier 1-1 draw with Dundee United for the Ibrox side, saw that the Celts, who started the month two points behind, finished it three points ahead despite the draw with Hibernian – and there were 10 games left to play.

There was more to this month with other SPFL wins over Motherwell, Aberdeen and Dundee delivering 13 goals in picking up those 12 points, and a 4-0 Scottish Cup victory over Raith Rovers while Giorgos Giakoumakis was coming to the fore, in the absence of the injured Kyogo, by netting a crucial hat-trick in the 3-2 win over Dundee.

Even defeat in the UEFA Europa Conference League to a stylish Bodø/Glimt was counteracted by the sea change in the league campaign as even a 0-0 draw in the final game at Easter Road came on the same day as Motherwell came from 2-0 down to draw 2-2 with Rangers.

MONTH'S MAGIC MOMENT

Guess? The difference between this night-time action under the Paradise lights and the daytime game at Ibrox was, well…night and day. Don't let the darkness fog your mind, though, this was nothing to do with the kick-off time, this turnaround had Ange Postecoglou's mind-set all over it.

The mixture of brand new incoming players and the group that he had moulded in the five intervening months since the last derby oozed confidence and skill as vibrant as the green and white Hoops they wore as they tore Rangers apart in a blistering first-half.

Among the new Bhoys was Reo Hatate, who owned the game by scoring twice and setting up Liel Abada for the other. If an entire game can be a game-changer, then this was it in terms of how the SPFL tide turned between the Southside and the East End of Glasgow.

SEASON REVIEW
HOW THE LEAGUE WAS WON
MARCH

ONLY half the games of the previous month, but all wins as the Celts stepped up the pressure with three SPFL victories and a win in the Scottish Cup keeping up the momentum.

Celtic dominated the opening game against St Mirren, but it wasn't until the second half that goals from Cameron Carter-Vickers and skipper, Callum McGregor gave the Hoops a 2-0 win. The opener was by Carter-Vickers from a Carl Starfelt challenge at a free-kick when the ball broke to the scorer.

The same partnership was to do the exact same the following month in a goal of even greater importance.

Next up was a trip to a difficult venue, but this time Celtic broke Livingston's resolve and a timely 3-1 win in West Lothian delivered another three points to the tally before Scottish Cup action resulted in a Monday night trip to Tannadice.

An opener from McGregor and a double from Giorgos Giakoumakis gave Celtic a 3-0 win and passage to the semi-final at Hampden, while the Greek striker kept up the scoring in the next game.

MONTH'S MATCHES

Comp	H/A	Date	Opponent	Result
SPFL	H	Wed 2 Mar	St Mirren	2-0 (Carter-Vickers 55, McGregor 81)
SPFL	A	Sun 6 Mar	Livingston	3-1 (Maeda 17, Devlin 46 og, Forrest 55)
SC	A	Mon 14 Mar	Dundee Utd	3-0 (McGregor 12, Giakoumakis 58, 88)
SPFL	H	Sat 19 Mar	Ross County	4-0 (Giakoumakis 11, 18, 61 pen, Maeda 26)

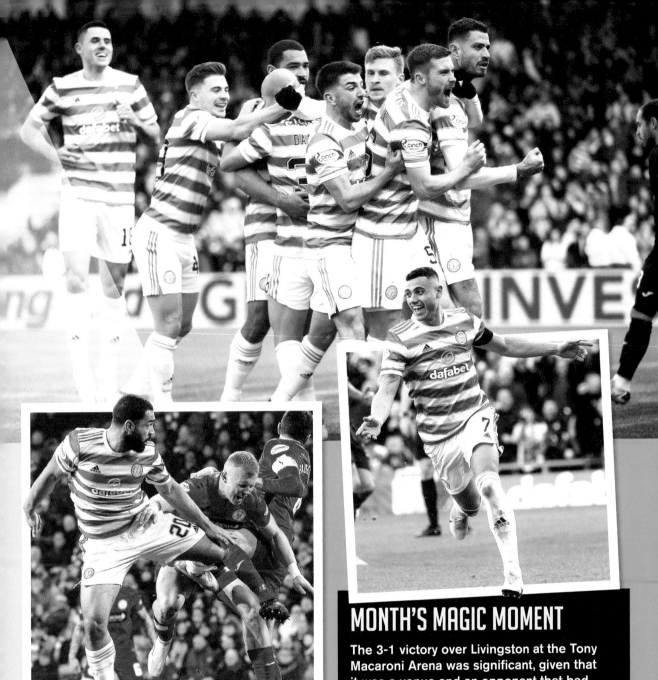

A ruthless Celtic, spearheaded by Giakoumakis, earned all three points in a clinical 4-0 win over Ross County. Giakoumakis completed a hat-trick from the spot, sending the keeper the wrong way to coolly slot into the bottom left for his second treble in his last five matches.

And, although Rangers won their three games as well, the nine Celtic league goals scored to Rangers' four bolstered the three-point lead with a goal difference of 14 into the bargain.

MONTH'S MAGIC MOMENT

The 3-1 victory over Livingston at the Tony Macaroni Arena was significant, given that it was a venue and an opponent that had proved to be extremely tough over the years. On the day, Ange Postecoglou's side were able to convert their dominance into goals.

That began in the 17th minute, not long after Callum McGregor missed a penalty, given for a handball inside the area, and it was Daizen Maeda who grabbed the all-important opener. Carl Starfelt's header from a Jota corner was saved, but the Japanese striker was on hand to head home on the line.

And a minute after the break, it was 2-0 when Nicky Devlin turned the ball into his own net from an Anthony Ralston cross.

James Forrest extended Celtic's lead on 55 minutes with a fine left-foot finish, and though Andrew Shinnie reduced the deficit a minute later, the Hoops saw out the game comfortably to take all three points.

SEASON REVIEW
HOW THE LEAGUE WAS WON
APRIL

CELTIC'S points' advantage doubled over the course of April with only three league games played and the fact that there were two derbies played, one successful and one lost, in the SPFL and Scottish Cup, lets you know who won the most important game.

Like February, this game kicked off with a derby, but this time it was at Ibrox with only 700 Hoops fans allowed in. However, despite the home side taking an early lead, the singing and dancing at the end was confined to those 700 who celebrated a 2-1 win.

This wasn't just any old 2-1 win, it stopped the Ibrox side from drawing level on points with the Hoops and, conversely, put Celtic six points ahead of their challengers.

The following weekend, 60,000 turned up at Celtic Park to carry on the celebrations and they were treated to the biggest win of the season as a very stylish Celtic side bamboozled St Johnstone with a 7-0 win that featured a 40+-pass move that ended with Matt O'Riley sweeping the ball home.

In the Scottish Cup semi-final, the Hoops took the lead through Greg Taylor, but

MONTH'S MATCHES

SPFL	A	Sun 3 Apr	Rangers	2-1 (Rogic 7, Carter-Vickers 42)
SPFL	H	Sat 9 Apr	St Johnstone	7-0 (Hatate 8, Giakoumakis 22, Maeda 36, Juranovic 51 pen, O'Riley 70, 73, Abada 78)
SC	N	Sun 17 Apr	Rangers	1-2 (Taylor 63) AET
SPFL	A	Sun 24 Apr	Ross County	2-0 (Kyogo 12, Jota 87)

MONTH'S MAGIC MOMENT

Cameron Carter-Vickers produced the winning strike as Celtic increased their lead to six points with a 2-1 win at Ibrox. Aaron Ramsey did give the hosts the lead after three minutes, but as had been shown throughout the season, Ange Postecoglou's side reacted to the early adversity, with first-half goals from Tom Rogic and then Carter-Vickers.

Just four minutes after the home side scored, Rogic had levelled. Callum McGregor did brilliantly to create space down the right wing and cut the ball back to Rogic in the box. His shot was deflected into the path of Reo Hatate and his effort was parried by Allan McGregor into the path of Rogic who side-footed home from close-range.

Then, three minutes from the break, a free-kick from Jota found the head of Carl Starfelt and his header was nodded into the path of Carter-Vickers who powered home a left-foot drive.

suffered extra-time heartache as Rangers progressed to the final.

Next up was a potentially dangerous trip to Ross County, but Jota was both goal-maker and goal-taker as he set up Kyogo for the opener and, late in the match, sealed the game, the three points and the six-point lead with a dramatic second as the Hoops finished the weekend as they had started it – six points ahead.

It wasn't all just about points by this time, though, as the Hoops also increased the goal difference to 19, basically an extra point, with only four games to play – and the first game of May would be another derby.

SEASON REVIEW
HOW THE LEAGUE WAS WON
MAY

IF the Hoops won the opener against Rangers, they could clinch the title the following weekend, a win for the Ibrox side would cut the lead to three points with three games to play, a draw would suit only one team – and that was Celtic – and that was the outcome.

Jota gave the Hoops a first-half lead, and though they created a number of other opportunities throughout the match, Celtic had to be content with a point after Fashion Sakala's second-half equaliser.

Hearts visited the following Saturday and Celtic took a massive step to the title with an impressive and noisy 4-1 win. Despite falling behind after three minutes, it was a near-perfect display, capped off by goals from Daizen Maeda, Kyogo, Matt O'Riley and Giorgos Giakoumakis and rounded off by an electric Celtic Park atmosphere.

That meant a point in the midweek trip to Tannadice to take on Dundee United would clinch the club's 10th title in 11 years – an amazing feat.

And the newly-crowned champions got there with the draw they needed thanks to

MONTH'S MATCHES

SPFL	H	Sun 1 May	Rangers	1-1 (Jota 20)
SPFL	H	Sat 7 May	Hearts	4-1 (Maeda 30, Kyogo 37, O'Riley 69, Giakoumakis 90)
SPFL	A	Wed 11 May	Dundee Utd	1-1 (Giakoumakis 53)
SPFL	H	Sat 14 May	Motherwell	6-0 (Kyogo 21, 44, Turnbull 40, Jota 59, Giakoumakis 68, 91)

WINNERS 2021/22
CELTIC FOOTBALL CLUB

MONTH'S MAGIC MOMENT

Take your pick – from either the header from Giorgos Giakoumakis that sealed the title, or the referee's final whistle in the same game at Tannadice that made everything official and cut and dried.

On the 53rd minute, the Greek striker powered home a header to give the Celts a 1-0 lead and inch them ever closer to becoming champions.

The work for the goal was made by Anthony Ralston, who jinked his way down the right wing before curling in a perfect cross for Giakoumakis at the back post and the 27-year-old leapt highest to slam his effort past Benjamin Siegrist.

It was a goal that was celebrated wildly at the time, even more so at the end of the game, and, of course the celebrations continued on Trophy Day come Saturday – *more of that over the page.*

a powerful header from Giakoumakis eight minutes after the break, and the equaliser in the 72nd minute only made the countdown to the title slightly more edgy but it didn't help delay the inevitable.

The Celtic fans inside Tannadice and the countless thousands watching live around the world erupted on the blow of the final whistle, knowing that 60,000 Celts would have a massive party just days later at Paradise.

There was still a job to be done, though, and Ange Postecoglou's Celts finished the league on a high as a resounding 6-0 win over Motherwell amid a party atmosphere ensured they had gone 32 games without defeat on the march to the title.

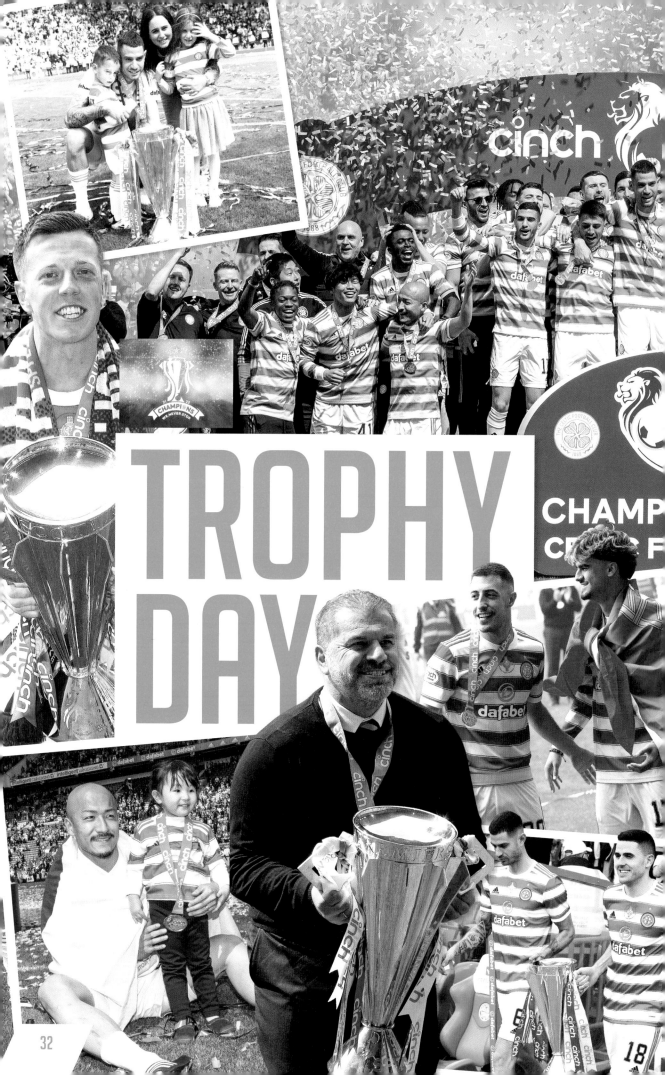

TROPHY DAY

33

CALLUM McGREGOR

Position: Midfielder

Squad Number: 42

D.O.B: 14/06/93

Born: Glasgow, Scotland

Height: 5'10"

Signed: 07/07/09

Debut: v KR Reykjavik (a) 1-0, (UCL) 15/07/14

Previous Clubs: Celtic Youth (on loan at Notts County while with Celtic)

JAMES FORREST

Position: Winger

Squad Number: 49

D.O.B: 07/07/91

Born: Prestwick, Scotland

Height: 5'9"

Signed: 01/07/09

Debut: v Motherwell (h) 4-0, (SPL) 01/05/10

Previous Clubs: Celtic Youth

JOE HART

Position: Goalkeeper

Squad Number: 1

D.O.B: 19/04/87

Born: Shrewsbury, England

Height: 6'5"

Signed: 03/08/21

Debut: v FK Jablonec (a) 4-2, (EL) 05/08/21

Previous Clubs: Tottenham Hotspur, Burnley, West Ham (loan), Torino (loan), Birmingham City (loan), Blackpool (loan), Tranmere Rovers (loan), Manchester City, Shrewsbury Town

LIEL ABADA

Position: Forward
Squad Number: 11
D.O.B: 03/10/01
Born: Petah Tikva, Israel
Height: 5'6"
Signed: 14/07/21
Debut: v FC Midtjylland (h) 1-1, (CL) 20/07/21
Previous Clubs: Maccabi Petah Tikva

KYOGO FURUHASHI

Position: Forward
Squad Number: 8
D.O.B: 20/01/95
Born: Nara, Japan
Height: 5'7"
Signed: 16/07/21
Debut: v Hearts (a) 1-2, (SPFL) 31/07/21
Previous Clubs: Vissel Kobe, FC Gifu

YOSUKE IDEGUCHI

Position: Midfielder
Squad Number: 21
D.O.B: 23/08/96
Born: Fukuoka, Japan
Height: 5'7"
Signed: 01/01/22
Debut: v Hibernian (h) 2-0, (SPFL) 17/01/22
Previous Clubs: Gamba Osaka, Greuther Fürth (loan), Cultural Leonesa (loan), Leeds United, J League U22 (loan), Gamba Osaka

CARL STARFELT

Position: Defender
Squad Number: 4
D.O.B: 01/06/95
Born: Stockholm, Sweden
Height: 6'1"
Signed: 26/07/21
Debut: v Hearts (a) 1-2, (SPFL) 31/07/21
Previous Clubs: Rubin Kazan, IFK Goteborg, IF Brommapojkarna

SCOTT BAIN

Position: Goalkeeper
Squad Number: 29
D.O.B: 22/11/91
Born: Edinburgh, Scotland
Height: 6'0"
Signed: 31/01/18
Debut: v Rangers (a) 3-2, (SPFL) 11/03/18
Previous Clubs: Hibernian (loan), Dundee, Alloa Athletic, Elgin City (loan), Aberdeen

MORITZ JENZ

Position: Defender
Squad Number: 6
D.O.B: 30/04/99
Born: Berlin, Germany
Height: 6'2"
Signed: 19/06/22
Debut: v Ross County (a) 3-1, (SPFL) 06/08/22
Previous Clubs: Lorient, Lausanne-Sport, Fulham, Tennis Borussia Berlin

SEAD HAKSABANOVIC

Position: Forward
Squad Number: 9
D.O.B: 04/05/99
Born: Hyltebruk, Sweden
Height: 5'9"
Signed: 25/08/22
Debut: v Ross County (a) 4-1, (LC) 31/08/22
Previous Clubs: Djurgardens IF (loan), Rubin Kazan, IFK Norrkoping (loan), Malaga (loan), West Ham United, Halmstads BK

OLIVER ABILDGAARD

Position: Midfielder
Squad Number: 28
D.O.B: 10/06/96
Born: Hasseris, Denmark
Height: 6'4"
Signed: 01/09/22
Debut: n/a*
Previous Clubs: Rubin Kazan, Aalborg BK

*Hadn't made debut at time of going to print.

ANTHONY RALSTON

Position: Defender

Squad Number: 56

D.O.B: 16/11/98

Born: Bellshill, Scotland

Height: 5'11"

Debut: v St Johnstone (a) 1-2, (SPFL) 11/05/16

Previous Clubs: Celtic Youth (on loan at Queen's Park, Dundee United and St Johnstone while with Celtic)

STEPHEN WELSH

Position: Defender

Squad Number: 57

D.O.B: 09/01/00

Born: Coatbridge, Scotland

Height: 5'9"

Signed: 01/07/18

Debut: v Hamilton Accies (a) 4-1, (SPFL) 02/02/20

Previous Clubs: Celtic Youth (on loan at Morton while with Celtic)

ALEXANDRO BERNABEI

Position: Defender

Squad Number: 25

D.O.B: 24/09/00

Born: Correa, Argentina

Height: 5'7"

Signed: 30/06/22

Debut: v Dundee United (a) 9-0, (SPFL) 28/08/22

Previous Clubs: Lanus

GREG TAYLOR

Position: Defender
Squad Number: 3
D.O.B: 05/11/97
Born: Greenock, Scotland
Height: 5'8"
Signed: 02/09/19
Debut: v St Mirren (h) 2-0, (SPFL) 30/10/19
Previous Clubs: Kilmarnock

BEN SIEGRIST

Position: Goalkeeper
Squad Number: 31
D.O.B: 31/01/92
Born: Therwil, Switzerland
Height: 6'4"
Signed: 21/06/22
Debut: v Ross County (a) 4-1, (LC) 31/08/22
Previous Clubs: Dundee United, Vaduz, Wycombe Wanderers (loan), Solihull Moors (loan), Cambridge United (loan), Burton Albion (loan), Aston Villa

JOSIP JURANOVIC

Position: Defender
Squad Number: 88
D.O.B: 16/08/95
Born: Zagreb, Croatia
Height: 5'8"
Signed: 21/08/21
Debut: v Rangers (a) 0-1, (SPFL) 29/08/21
Previous Clubs: Legia Warsaw, Hajduk Split, Dubrava

SCOTT ROBERTSON

Position: Midfielder

Squad Number: 35

D.O.B: 27/07/01

Born: Lenzie, Scotland

Height: 5'9"

Signed: 24/07/19

Debut: v CFR Cluj (a) 0-2, (EL) 12/12/19

Previous Clubs: Celtic Youth
(on loan at Gillingham, Doncaster Rovers
and Crewe Alexandria while at Celtic)

JAMES McCARTHY

Position: Midfielder

Squad Number: 16

D.O.B: 12/11/90

Born: Glasgow, Scotland

Height: 5'11"

Signed: 03/08/21

Debut: v Hearts (h) 3-2, (LC) 15/08/21

Previous Clubs: Hamilton Accies, Wigan
Athletic, Everton, Crystal Palace

GIORGOS GIAKOUMAKIS

Position: Forward

Squad Number: 7

D.O.B. 09/12/94

Born: Heraklion, Greece

Height: 6'1"

Signed: 31/08/21

Debut: v Bayer Leverkusen (h) 0-4 (EL), 30/09/21

Previous Clubs: VVV-Venlo, AEK Athens,
Gornik Zabrze (loan), OFI (loan), Platanias,
Episkopi (loan), Atsalenios

JOAO FILIPE JOTA

Position: Forward
Squad Number: 17
D.O.B: 30/03/99
Born: Lisbon, Portugal
Height: 5'9''
Signed: 31/08/21
Debut: v Ross County (h) 3-0 SPFL, 11/09/21
Previous Clubs: Valladolid (loan), Benfica

CAMERON CARTER-VICKERS

Position: Defender
Squad Number: 20
D.O.B: 31/12/97
Born: Southend-on-Sea, England
Height: 6'
Signed: 31/08/21
Debut: v Ross County (h) 3-0 SPFL, 11/09/21
Previous Clubs: AFC Bournemouth (loan), Luton Town (loan), Stoke City (loan), Swansea City (loan), Ipswich Town (loan), Sheffield United (loan), Tottenham Hotspur

MATT O'RILEY

Position: Midfielder
Squad Number: 33
D.O.B: 21/11/00
Born: Hounslow, England
Height: 6'2''
Signed: 21/01/22
Debut: v Hearts (a) 2-1, (SPFL) 26/01/22
Previous Clubs: Milton Keynes Dons, Fulham

DAIZEN MAEDA

Position: Forward
Squad Number: 38
D.O.B: 20/10/97
Born: Osaka, Japan
Height: 5'8''
Signed: 01/01/22
Debut: v Hibernian (h) 2-0, (SPFL) 17/01/22
Previous Clubs: Yokohama F Marinos, Maritimo (loan), Mito Hollyhock (loan), Matsumoto Yamaga

REO HATATE

Position: Midfielder

Squad Number: 41

D.O.B: 21/11/97

Born: Suzuka, Mie, Japan

Height: 5'8''

Signed: 01/01/22

Debut: v Hibernian (h) 2-0, (SPFL) 17/01/22

Previous Clubs: Kawasaki Frontale

DAVID TURNBULL

Position: Midfielder

Squad Number: 14

D.O.B: 10/07/99

Born: Carluke, Scotland

Height: 6'1''

Signed: 27/08/20

Debut: v Ross County (a) 5-0, (SPFL) 12/09/20

Previous Clubs: Motherwell

AARON MOOY

Position: Midfielder

Squad Number: 13

D.O.B: 15/09/90

Born: Sydney, Australia

Height: 5'9''

Signed: 19/06/22

Debut: v Aberdeen (h) 2-0, (SPFL) 31/07/22

Previous Clubs: Shanghai Port, Brighton, Huddersfield Town, Manchester City, Melbourne City, Western Sydney Wanderers, St Mirren, Bolton Wanderers

THE GHIRLS' HISTORIC CUP DOUBLE PART 1....

Celtic Women buck the trend to lift the League Cup

BACK in 2010, Celtic FC Women reached the final of the SWPL Cup for the first time and beat Spartans 4-1 to lift their first silverware.

It was the ninth final of the competition and the first not to feature either Glasgow City or Hibernian, although the previous year's final was the only one of the nine to feature both of those sides facing each other, and in facing the Hoops, the unlucky Spartans were appearing as losing finalists for the second of five times in six years.

In the nine finals played since Celtic's win (two seasons were missed due to Covid), only Hibs (five times) and Glasgow City (four times) have lifted the trophy since then, and both also managed four-in-a-row during that period.

The two middle wins of Hibernian's four-in-a-row, 2017 and 2018, were both against Celtic. This was a hopeful sign that the tide was slowly turning in Scottish Women's football as the Easter Road outfit had traditionally been the only viable challengers to City's dominance in league football over the piece.

As far as the League Cup goes, there had only been four winners prior to this season's final, with Hibs winning seven to City's six, inaugural winners Kilmarnock lifting it three times, and Edinburgh (who became Spartans) winning it once.

SCOTTISH WOMEN'S PREMIER LEAGUE CUP

MATCH FACTS
SWPL Cup Final
Sunday, December 5, 2021
Firhill Stadium, Glasgow
CELTIC 1
(Hayes 25)
GLASGOW CITY 0

Indeed, aside from the six teams already mentioned in final meetings – Celtic, Hibernian, Glasgow City, Kilmarnock, Edinburgh and Spartans – only two more teams have even reached any of the 19 finals played so far – Raith Rovers and Queen's Park Ladies.

So when Celtic FC Women took to the field at Firhill on December 5 to face Glasgow City in the 19th SWPL Cup final, they were aiming to be the first to break the Hibs/City duopoly since 2010 when the Hoops last won by becoming only the fifth club to lift the trophy.

They would be facing a side who had lifted the league title 14 times in succession on top of their SWPL Cup and other silverware successes – clearly a team who were used to winning.

However, Celtic tore up the script and only the City goalkeeper stopped the Hoops from reaching a far more convincing scoreline, but Caitlin Hayes' strong header from a Sarah Harkes free-kick in the 25th minute was enough to lift the first available silverware of the season – and there would be more to come from Fran Alonso's side…

See pages 52/53 for Part 2 of the story…

TO say there was a bit of an Aussie input to Celtic's successes last season in both the men's and women's teams would be a bit of an understatement.

You don't have to be Aussie detective Jack Irish to work out what Ange Postecoglou brought to the table last season, then there was Tom Rogic on the pitch delivering as usual when it really mattered, and one of the many stars of the women's best-ever season was Jacynta Galabadaarachchi.

The fact that both Ange and Jacynta each picked up national individual awards away from the club perfectly illustrates their input and impact – the boss picking up Manager of the Year at both the PFA Scotland (players) and SFWA (writers) ceremonies, and Jacynta the PFA Scotland Women's Young Player of the Year.

And, just when it looked like the Aussie contingent would be sliced with the departure of Rogic, up stepped Harry Kewell as first-team coach back in June, soon to be joined by midfielder, Aaron Mooy in July.

He said at the time: "It is a massive honour to join Celtic and team up with Ange. He and his backroom team and the players have done brilliantly in their first year together, producing winning football in a great style. To turn things around and become champions so quickly is a huge testament to Ange and everyone else at the club.

"The manager is synonymous with attacking, exciting football, something he delivered on last season and something I know Celtic fans have loved right across the generations. We will be aiming to give our fans more of the same going forward and I look forward to playing my part in bringing this to our supporters."

Also, it hasn't always been one-way traffic with the likes of Dixie Deans moving to play in Australia in the 1970s, and others like early 1960s 'keeper Frank Haffey, Lisbon Lion Willie Wallace and club legend Paul McStay all having made Australia their home after moving Down Under.

However, the very first Australian to play for the Hoops actually didn't travel halfway around the world to get here, and he didn't travel back there when he left Celtic – in fact he never kicked a ball in earnest in Australia. Dan Lavery was born in Sydney in 1925 to an Irish family, but they returned home when he was very young and he was brought up in Ballynahinch where he grew up to play Gaelic football as well as soccer.

Indeed, he joined Celtic from Antrim GAA and scored on his debut against Hibernian in 1948, but that was one of only four appearances before he moved back to Ireland and Ballymena United in 1949.

That was the only Aussie input until Melbourne-born Will Hastie arrived in 1989 as a 16-year-old from a Celtic-daft family, but, although he was on his way by 1991, he was the first Aussie at Celtic to be rather unimaginatively nicknamed 'Skippy' by his team-mates.

He had a short spell at Dundee, but was signed by Willie McStay at Sligo Rovers and became a hero in their treble-winning 1993/94 side before returning to play in Australia where he then became involved in the Australian PFA.

AUSSIES RULE....

...with Ange, and Jacynta and Harry Kewell

Next up was Mark Viduka, another Melburnian born and bred, but this time from a Croatian family, hence him joining Celtic from Dinamo Zagreb in 1998. Although he departed in 2000, there was only one full season with the Hoops and he scored 35 goals in 46 games before joining Leeds United.

Another Aussie Celt was born into a Celtic family in the Melbourne suburb of Dandenong, and that was Scott McDonald and, as a youngster he was at Gippsland Falcons while Will Hastie was a first-team player there. The striker joined Celtic from Motherwell in 2007, and before departing in 2010 to join Middlesbrough, he had scored 64 goals in 128 games while also lifting league and League Cup winning medals.

Another Aussie to arrive as a youth player was another Melburnian, Jackson Irvine, who arrived in 2012 and captained the youth side to a league and cup double. The Youth Cup win was the middle one of three he helped win.

However, he only played one first-team game, coming on as a sub in a 2-2 draw with Hibernian in September 2012, although he played around 30 times each for Kilmarnock and Ross County on loan before joining the Dingwall side permanently in 2015.

That brings us to Tom Rogic, easily the Aussie that has made the biggest impact at Celtic – well, as a player at least. The same age as Irvine, the midfielder, who was born in Griffith near Canberra, arrived just as his fellow Australian was gaining experience on loan, but while Rogic also went on loan back Down Under with Melbourne Victory, he would have rather more success.

In terms of longevity and medal haul, Rogic outstrips all of his fellow Aussie counterparts and after 46 goals in 273 games in his Celtic spell between 2012/13 and 2021/22, the classy midfielder left with no fewer than **SIXTEEN** top-level winner's medals – six SPFL, five Scottish Cups and five League Cups.

PARADISE PUZZLES!

SPOT THE DIFFERENCE

THERE are 10 differences between these two photographs of the Celtic Ghirls celebrating their 3-2 Scottish Cup win over Glasgow City at Tynecastle.
The first one has been circled, but can you spot the rest?

WHO DID WHAT?

Can you link the Celt to the clue?

HARRY KEWELL

GIORGOS GIAKOUMAKIS

I've represented both my hometown football and cricket clubs.

I have lifted league titles for the past three years.

CALLUM McGREGOR

I once played for the world's oldest professional football club.

ANGE POSTECOGLOU

I used to play for a team that has a shamrock as their emblem.

JOE HART

I played for a team managed by a former Celt who also managed Scotland.

My country has a medal in my name presented to the best Under-23 player.

CARL STARFELT

My international debut was against the country where I played my club football.

REO HATATE

I was born in the same town as the Celtic 2012/13 Player of the Year.

My very first club wore the Hoops.

CAMERON CARTER-VICKERS

YOSUKE IDEGUCHI

I played for a team that once lost successive FA Cup finals to Blackburn Rovers.

ANTHONY RALSTON

2021/22 QUIZ

Were you paying attention during the season?

1. Who was Celtic's top scorer in the SPFL?

2. And who was the club's top scorer all round?

3. How many SPFL clean sheets did Joe Hart have?

4. Quickly, his forename begins and ends with the same letter, and another letter also begins and ends his surname, which Celt is this?

5. What three teams did Celtic beat 6-0?

6. When Celtic lifted the League Cup, how many times had they now lifted the trophy?

7. Which two Celts played 54 times in all competitions?

8. How many of Celtic's home SPFL matches produced clean sheets for the Hoops?

9. Joey Dawson made his debut this season, but against which side?

10. Kyogo was replaced from the bench by which Celt in the League Cup final?

Answers on pages 62/63

SHOOTING-STAR CELTS

Magnificent Seven from the Hoops delivers the side's highest scoreline of 2021/22

CELTIC'S biggest win of the 2021/22 season was the magnificent 7-0 SPFL win over St Johnstone which came just a week after the Hoops really stated their title intentions with a 2-1 win at Ibrox, and this goal spree against the Perth side showed that Ange Postecoglou's side weren't for slipping up.

The victory was also Celtic's biggest win since beating the same team in the same competition on August 3, 2019, and even though it was only two-and-a-half years earlier, the only scorer from that game still at the club was Mikey Johnston. He opened the scoring in the ninth minute while Ryan Christie (3), Olivier Ntcham, Odsonne Edouard and Leigh Griffiths also found the net. In this game, however, the seven goals were spread between six players – all Ange signings – and here's how the scoring unfolded.

No.2
A Josip Juranovic pass seemed to be covered by Callum Booth, but incessant pressing by the speedy Daizen Maeda forced a hurried pass-back and Giorgos Giakoumakis pounced to slot home from the tightest of angles.

No.1
A second phase of a wonderful passing display in the box ended with a Reo Hatate shot, to open the scoring for the Hoops.

MATCH FACTS
SPFL
Saturday, April 9, 2022
Celtic Park
CELTIC 7
(Hatate 8, Giakoumakis 22, Maeda 36, Juranovic 51 (pen), O'Riley 70, 73, Abada 78)
ST JOHNSTONE 0

No.3
Unfortunately, Giako had to depart soon after with an injury, but the pressure was maintained and a pinpoint cross on the left from Jota was perfectly placed for Maeda to nod home the third.

No.4
This came from the spot when Juranovic coolly slotted away from 12 yards six minutes after the break when Hatate was bundled down in the box.

No.5
This was the first from substitute Matt O'Riley who got his head to a David Turnbull cross.

No.6
The new Danish Under-21 internationalist was on the scoresheet again just three minutes later when he produced deft footwork and fired in No.6 from the edge of the box following a multi-pass move.

No.7
A wonderful ball from Kyogo fell perfectly for Maeda who touched for Liel Abada, and it was the Israeli who fired in the final goal with a stylish shot… cue the theme tune from The Magnificent Seven once more.

ANGE'S HAMPDEN HEROES

THIS was Celtic's opportunity to lift the League Cup for the 20th time, and, if they did, Ange Postecoglou would get his hands on the trophy for the very first time – at the very first time of asking.

CELTIC and Hibernian had met in three previous League Cup finals prior to this 2021/22 showdown, and two hefty scorelines from the Hoops sandwiched the one win by the capital club over the Hoops.

In season 1968/69, a Bobby Lennox hat-trick helped the Hoops to a 6-2 win over the Edinburgh side – this was the season that the Celts wrapped up all three elements of the Treble in an amazing 21-day period, this April 5 final being the first of the trio.

Just three years later, Hibs gained some measure of revenge when an excellent Easter Road side beat Celtic 2-1 at Hampden.

Then, in season 1974/75, there was hat-trick action again in this Battle of the Greens League Cup final – for both sides. Joe Harper netted a triple for Hibs, but, unfortunately for

him, Dixie Deans did the same for Celtic as he contributed half the team's goals in a 6-3 final win.

So, Hibs could level the League Cup final tally between the sides if they could overcome the Celts at the National Stadium and, in the 50th minute, they took a reasonable step towards that possibility when Paul Hanlon put them in front.

The Hibs fans were still celebrating the goal, however, when the noise level abruptly switched ends as Kyogo Furuhashi levelled the tie almost immediately.

Then, in the 71st minute, the Japanese striker hit the spot again with a delightful volley that looped over the helpless keeper and into the net.

This time the noise level wouldn't switch ends and the first piece of Ange Postecoglou silverware for the season would soon be on its way back to Paradise on the Celtic team bus.

THE GHIRLS' HISTORIC CUP DOUBLE PART 2...

Celtic Women defy the odds again to lift the Scottish Cup

ALTHOUGH a much older competition than the SWPL Cup, the Scottish Women's Cup, which started in season 1970/71, has had a very similar history to its younger League Cup counterpart since around the formation of the SWPL in 2002/03.

Indeed, the Scottish Cup in the two seasons before the inauguration of the SWPL had been won by Kilmarnock, who were winners of the League Cup for the first two seasons of its existence and, in fact, in their previous incarnation of Stewarton, that club lifted the very first Scottish Cup in 1970/71.

Since season 2002/03, however, the Scottish Cup has been steadfastly in the hands of either Hibernian or Glasgow City – very much mirroring their influence on the destination of the League Cup.

Prior to this season, like the League Cup, two tournaments were missed because of Covid, but the 17 finals contested since 2002/03 have all been won by either Hibs or City, with the capital club winning eight, the Glasgow outfit nine, including five-in-a-row.

No fewer than seven of those finals featured those sides playing against each other, Hibs winning three and City the other four, while only nine other sides had managed to reach the final over the course of that period.

MATCH FACTS

Scottish Women's Cup final
Sunday, May 29, 2022
Tynecastle Park, Edinburgh
CELTIC 3
(Shen 19, Wellings 35 pen, Atkinson 114)
GLASGOW CITY 2
(Clark 25, Davidson 40 pen)
(AET 2-2 90 minutes)

Biffa
SCOTTISH WOM[E]'S CUP

Among those nine was Celtic, who came closest to Scottish Cup success in the 2008 final when they took Hibs to extra-time but lost 3-1 at the end of the day.

However, could Celtic repeat their earlier League Cup success against Glasgow City at Firhill when they met them again in the 2021/22 Scottish Cup final at Tynecastle?

To do that, they would have to break the 17-final hegemony of the two leading lights of Scottish women's football for the past two decades.

Like Celtic's last Scottish Cup final, this one also went to extra-time and, despite everything seeming to go against the Hoops, they persevered for the very final game of the season and despite being at a numerical disadvantage for over 80 minutes, they lifted their very first Scottish Cup.

Chinese star, Shen Mengu fired the Hoops ahead in the 19th minute, only for City to equalise barely six minutes later.

Top-scorer Charlie Wellings notched her 40th goal of the term in the 35th minute from the spot with a coolly-taken penalty, but, the same award a few minutes later at the other end not only saw City level again, but Jodie Bartle was harshly sent off and the Celts were down to 10.

The 10 Celts would not be beaten, though, even when the final went to a strength-sapping 30 minutes of extra-time, but a lovely turn by Sarah Harkes in the 114th minute saw her thread the ball through to substitute, Izzy Atkinson, and she calmly placed her shot through the legs of the keeper for the winner.

Atkinson's goal not only sealed Celtic's first Scottish Cup, but also clinched the Ghirls' first Cup Double.

53

PARADISE PUZZLES!

SCORER WORDSEARCH

HIDDEN in this word grid are just 20 of the many Celtic goalscorers who regularly found the net for the Hoops down through the years, so see how many you can find. You might want to get your parents or even grandparents involved in this game as well!

```
R C H Z D E S T K Y I H O E A M Y E N T H P P F B
K M E F I I U F Q W M U L D J J E M U F A U R O Z
P D N F O C X K H W F E D I M E Q Q G P R R B U T
D G R R T H N I A W B J M S R H D Z E V R B I T C
R R I V E G J W E M M M K Y R O R G C M Y M M I J
A R K Q B H I O E D Y W Y O L W E F Z L H A I I I
U H L M R H C D E Q E O D E N J U F E S O K R F W
O O A M Q A A A U M N A K T V T Y N T V O A H B H
D Y R W Y S G I L U C V N F E R N X D Z D J H U G
E X S Q S M N R X L Q B U S R O A K K B U L R Z L
E B S U T N Z M I A A G R M X E O G S T E B N W Q
N W O N V E R J B K G G V I W G P C C C V T D K J
N M N L J T T F F L E P Y P D I E O A M Q G V R X
O J L O N E X Q F H I M K S L E D L O N K V H K W
S Z I U O D B I X C O B F J T I L N L H V N Q F X
D J N M S A B R I A N M C C L A I R P P Y Y A U C
O E D A T C C M C K A Y P F W K P J D V P R L R S
K Y L C R E Y U I O H V R E D B H R T D K G A P F
O A R A A G X A F T O Q I G D L Q E C T I D B G I
T I R R H R J O M K N L M M K R X H D G F F K R V
G Y T I N O D I W T L E I N N E V A C M K N A R F
O S W G H J Z P Z I R D M G H B A J I U G F G C V
C M X K O K U T W B J R J P P F P C I B U N C G J
A N O E J Q G G H V S T E V I E C H A L M E R S D
K J S O D F Y T H S I L G L A D Y N N E K P N L H
```

Henrik Larsson	Bobby Lennox	Jimmy McGrory	Gary Hooper
Odsonne Edouard	Moussa Dembele	Stevie Chalmers	Dixie Deans
Harry Hood	Jimmy Quinn	Kenny Dalglish	Patsy Gallacher
John Hartson	Willie Wallace	Brian McClair	Joe McBride
Lou Macari	Frank McAvennie	Frank McGarvey	Jorge Cadete

SPOT THE BALL

KYOGO is just about to fire in a goal in the 6-0 Trophy Day win over Motherwell. There are six match balls in this pic of him about to score, but only one of them is the real one. Can you spot which one it is?

CELTIC PLAYER OF WHAT YEAR?

HERE we have half-a-dozen former Celtic Players of the Year and six seasons from the past two decades. Can you connect the Hoops star to the season he was voted the top Celt by the supporters?

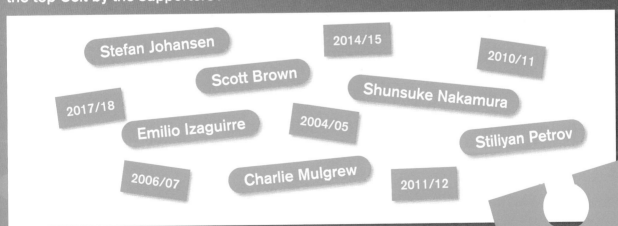

Stefan Johansen

2014/15

2010/11

Scott Brown

2017/18

Shunsuke Nakamura

Emilio Izaguirre

2004/05

Stiliyan Petrov

2006/07

Charlie Mulgrew

2011/12

Answers on pages 62/63

CELTS' SILVER SEASON

How 2021/22 went for Fran Alonso and the Ghirls

JUST as the Celtic men's side experienced an early season of change, upheaval, new singings, expectancy and, ultimately, silverware success, the club's women's side charted a very similar path and mirrored their bigger brothers with a double trophy win as a reward for a more than memorable season.

The season started with the women's team's first ever venture into continental competitive football as they took their first steps into UEFA Champions League football, and it ended on the last day with the side's very first Scottish Cup win played in front of the country's record crowd for a final in Scottish women's football.

The only difference from the men's team at the start of the campaign was that Ange Postecoglou was starting with a completely clean slate as a new incoming manager, while Fran Alonso already had a couple of years to settle in and get his message across, but he still had his work cut out and wasn't slow in bringing in new faces.

The frame of the team was still there to build around with captain Kelly Clark ably backed by other stalwarts of the side that qualified for European football like Chloe Craig and Natalie Ross.

Also in the mix were goalkeeping duo Chloe Logan and Rachael Johnstone, while other team members such as Sarah Harkes, Caitlin Hayes, Tegan Bowie and

Jodie Bartle had been joined in early 2021 by Jacynta Galabadaarachchi.

The new 2021/22 season, though, like the men's team, brought new faces with a more than international feel about the side as players arrived from around the world to join the Spanish manager at Celtic FC Women.

From China came Shen Mengyu, María Ólafsdóttir Gros arrived from Iceland while North America was represented by Cheyenne Shorts of the USA and Canadian Clarissa Larisey, and New Zealand midfielder Olivia Chance also arrived.

From closer to home, Irish Ghirl Tyler Toland who had been on loan from Manchester City signed a permanent deal and she would soon be joined by fellow Irishwoman Annie Timoney while, amid a goalkeeping injury crisis, Scots-born Maltese internationalist Anna Vincenti joined.

Last but not least from the closer-to-home signings was Charlie Wellings who made the trip up from south of the border and proceeded to smash in 40 goals in only 34 games to become the country's top scorer for the season.

The team was further bolstered at the start of this 2022/23 season when Kelly Clark, Caitlin Hayes, Chloe Craig and Jacynta all committed their immediate future to the club by signing new deals following their dramatic and historic Cup Double.

And the work didn't stop there as Amy Gallacher from Hibernian and Lucy Ashworth Clifford from Lewes became the first signings of the close season as the strengthening of the side continued.

That close season, though, provided a very well-earned break for the Ghirls after their 2021/22 Cup Double feat.

The League Cup was lifted in December at Firhill with a 1-0 win over Glasgow City after defeating Rangers (1-0), then holders Hibernian (2-1) to get there – not an easy road to take by any manner of means.

The Scottish Cup arrived in May with City defeated 3-2 this time after extra-time, and the road to this final included games against Edinburgh City (12-0), Rangers (2-1), Aberdeen (2-0) and Hearts (2-0 after extra time).

It wasn't only team achievements that illustrated just how far the team travelled last season as Jacynta also became PFA Scotland's very first winner of the Women's Young Player of the Year to add to also lifting the Celtic Women's Player of the Year on the same night.

All in all, it was a great and memorable season for Fran Alonso and his Ghirls as it doesn't get much better than lifting the League Cup for the first time in 12 years and then doubling that up with the Scottish Cup for the first time ever in a Cup Double whammy.

PICTURE THIS...

Celtic's 2021/22 Japanese story

ONE of the most endearing and satisfying photos of the entire 2021/22 season was, like many, taken on the final day of the league campaign.

It's of the Celtic's Japanese contingent, Yosuke Ideguchi, Kyogo Furuhashi, Reo Hatate and Daizen Maeda along with some family members sitting on the hallowed turf in the Paradise sun, and they look for all the world as if they are posing for a pic on a family picnic.

Also gleaming amid them, though, is the SPFL trophy bedecked in green and white cinch ribbons and 120,000 eyes are taking in the scene from the stands.

When Ange Postecoglou arrived in June after working wonders in the J League with Yokohama F Marinos, there was already talk of his knowledge of the Japanese scene being utilised by the club and, even then, certain players were being pinpointed in connection with the Hoops from media in both hemispheres.

That was all 11 months before the 'family photo' was snapped, and if ever a photo affirmed and encapsulated the manager's signing policy and relentlessness, then this was it.

Not only did this quartet contain four very skilful individual players, not only were they successful in applying themselves as part of a very successful silverware-winning Celtic side, but they were clearly happy and settled as well, perfectly content being a Celt. And that is always a chief consideration when Ange Postecoglou is signing a player from anywhere in the world, be it Aberdeen or Argentina – he is signing the man, the person, not just the footballer.

There had been Japanese footballers at Celtic before, Shunsuke Nakamura is an out-and-out Celtic legend following his stay between 2005 and 2009, while Koki Mizuno also tried his hand with the Hoops between 2008 and 2010.

However, 2021/22 was different – very different – and all four J League players along with the other new Celts brought in by the manager from around the world slotted seamlessly into a side that wouldn't give up until it won the title – a side that never stopped.

Kyogo was the first to arrive in July 2021 and after coming on as a sub against Hearts, he scored in his first start, a 4-2 away European win over FK Jablonec before returning three days later for his first game at Paradise – and he smashed that one with a hat-trick in a 6-0 win over Dundee.

The striker very quickly became a fans' favourite, and it would be no surprise if that season's League Cup final comes to be known as the 'Kyogo Final' among Hoops fans as his two excellently taken goals turned the game on its head after Hibernian had taken the lead.

Come the winter transfer window, there was no grass growing under Ange Postecoglou's feet as, well before the transfer deadline, the Celtic faithful knew that Yosuke Ideguchi, Reo Hatate and Daizen Maeda were joining the club.

Yosuke arrived having worn the hoops before – the green and white hoops of German side Greuther Furth – and looked forward to wearing the Celtic Hoops. Injury played its part in keeping him out of the running for much of the second half of the season but he returned to play alongside his Japanese colleagues on the day the Celts lifted the SPFL trophy.

That took him to six games, all victories with the Celts scoring 19 goals for the loss of only one – ironically to lower-league Alloa Athletic in the Scottish Cup.

His fellow Japanese January signings made their debuts in the same Hibernian game as Yosuke, and Hatate would really burst on to the scene in the next Premiership game against the other Edinburgh side – Hearts away at Tynecastle when his blockbuster of a shot paved the way to a 2-1 win.

However, even that was eclipsed by his stunning double in the first derby of 2022 and he also set up Liel Abada for the other in a classic 3-0 win.

He wasn't as quick off the mark as Maeda, who only took less than five minutes into that Hibernian debut to announce his arrival with his first Celtic goal – and an iconic goal celebration was born.

That was the first of eight times we saw that goal celebration which was an impersonation of Japanese anime character Anpanman who his young daughter also mimics… and the wee one brings us right back to the iconic photo.

Every Celtic picture tells a Celtic story.

FROM ACADEMY TO CAPTAIN

Callum McGregor shows how it's done

IF you had to choose a player to illustrate to a young Celtic Academy player just how far they could go in the game, you needn't look any further than Callum McGregor.

What would a young Academy player dream of in the Hoops? Certainly making his first-team debut, maybe even scoring on his debut – surely the dream of every young hopeful.

Then going on to consolidate your place in the first team as part of a group of players who would not only lift enough silverware to sink a pirate galleon, but would include historic and record-breaking trophy wins – including scoring in the odd final here and there.

Maybe even score in successive derby victories against your rivals, that helps propel you into the upper echelons of the club's greatest medal winners – we're talking Lisbon Lion territory here folks.

It would be remiss not to consider Player of the Year awards and playing for your country, then, why not be greedy and dream about captaining the team while the silverware keeps rolling in.

Callum McGregor has done it all and there is still more to come from the leader on the pitch who last season captained the Celts to the SPFL title and the League Cup in his first season as skipper.

Winning a trophy at the National Stadium is nothing new to the Hoops skipper, indeed he was no stranger to scoring in finals there even as a teenager.

It was only 10 years ago that he was taking part in his fourth successive Youth Cup final – he helped win them all, and in the third of those, he scored a hat-trick in an 8-0 final win over Queen of the South at Hampden, in a team coached by none other than current first-team coach, John Kennedy.

That hat-trick was scored as an 18-year-old, meaning he played in his first Youth Cup final as a 15-year-old.

You can also throw in a couple of successive SPL Under-19 League championships during that four-year cup-winning run.

It was as an eight-year-old that he joined the Academy set-up back in 2001, and (pictured here with the Under-11s) he has gone from strength to strength ever since – the cream of the crop always rises to the top.

He did, of course, score on his first-team debut and the rest of those dreams listed above became reality for the midfielder who took over the club captaincy from another Hoops hero, Scott Brown, at the start of last season.

He said on becoming captain: "I just try to keep leading in the way that I have done alongside Scott before, and now I will be the man to take those responsibilities. It's another challenge for me as well, the next stage in my development as a person and as a player, so it's something I am looking forward to.

"It's something every player should do anyway in terms of having that responsibility of being a first-team player. You become responsible for the results of the team and your part within the team, so it's an obvious responsibility but more so when you have the title of being the captain – more of it falls on you.

"But as a professional footballer anyway, you get used to dealing with the expectation to win and setting standards within the building which can drive a winning culture."

And after leading the Celts to two trophies, he said: "It was about me putting my personality into the role, but you need good players and people with you to make you a success and that's why we've done as well as a group."

This is, indeed, the stuff that dreams are made of.

PARADISE PUZZLE ANSWERS

PAGE 46: SPOT THE DIFFERENCE

PAGE 47: WHO DID WHAT?

I once played for the world's oldest professional football club.
Callum McGregor who was on loan at Notts County.

I used to play for a team that has a shamrock as their emblem.
Yosuke Ideguchi who spent time on loan at German side Greuther Furth who wear green and white
Hoops with a shamrock badge.

I have lifted league titles for the past three years.
Reo Hatate who won the J League with Kawasaki Frontale in 2020 and 2021, and then lifted the 2021/22
SPFL title with Celtic.

I played for a team managed by a former Celt who also managed Scotland.
Ange Postecoglou as a youngster when Tommy Docherty managed South Melbourne.

I've represented both my hometown football and cricket clubs.
Joe Hart who has played for both Shrewsbury Town FC and Shrewsbury Cricket Club.

My very first club wore the Hoops.
Cameron Carter-Vickers who started with Catholic United on Southend-on-Sea.

My country has a medal in my name presented to the best Under-23 player.
The Harry Kewell Medal has been presented to the best A-League or overseas-based Australian since 2009.

My international debut was against the country where I played my club football.
Carl Starfelt made his debut for Sweden against Russia when he played there with Rubin Kazan.

I was born in the same town as the Celtic 2012/13 Player of the Year.
Giorgos Giakoumakis and Georgios Samaras were both born in Heraklion, Crete.

I played for a team that once lost successive FA Cup finals to Blackburn Rovers.
Anthony Ralston has been on loan at Queen's Park, and in the early days of football, Scottish clubs
could also play in the FA Cup. The Glasgow club got to the final in 1884 and 1885 and lost 2-1
and 2-0 at Kennington Oval.